Contents

ACKNOWLEDGMENTS
I am deeply indebted to James A. Borland and Ronald E. Hawkins for their assistance in editing my sermons on the Book of Proverbs from which the text of this book was taken. Also, recognition is due Marie Chapman for editorial assistance and to Jody, Lois, and Nanine for typing the manuscript.

INTRODUCTION

The Book of Proverbs belongs to the poetic books of the Old Testament and, in particular to the section known as the wisdom literature. A proverb is a "wise saying" that summarizes a great truth into a simple thought. For example: "He that troubleth his own house shall inherit the wind" (11:29) teaches the importance of parental example. The majority of the proverbs were written by Solomon in the tenth century B.C. They represent the way of wisdom as the way to spiritual success.

The purpose of a proverb is to clarify and emphasize truth in such a way that it can be remembered easily. A modern proverb says, "An apple a day keeps the doctor away." The biblical proverbs are expressions of the wisdom of God. They teach moral values, principles of practical living, warn against the destructiveness of sin, and encourage spiritual diligence. In general, the Book of Proverbs teaches a "better way" to live. For example: "For wisdom is *better* than rubies" (8:11).

Following typical Hebrew poetic structure, the proverbs are written in both synonymous and antithetical parallels. For example: "Pride goeth before destruction, and a haughty spirit before a fall" (16:18) or, "Hatred stirreth up strifes, but love covereth all sins" (10:12). Some proverbs promise blessings. For example: "Train up a child in the way he should go, and when he is old, he will not depart from it" (22:6). Other proverbs warn of judgment, such as, "He that soweth iniquity shall reap vanity, and the rod of his anger shall fail" (22:8).

Knowledge is the accumulation of facts and information, whereas, wisdom is the practical application of those facts. One need not be a scholar or an intellectual in order to have wisdom. God is the author of wisdom and all who trust in Him can learn to be wise and discerning Christians. As you study Proverbs, let God develop His wisdom in your soul. Do not be content with learning the truth but rather learn how to live the truth.

Jerry Falwell

DEDICATION
To my dear departed mother, Helen,
who lived and taught the principles
expounded in the Book of Proverbs.

1
The Path
to Success
Proverbs 1

Symbols of knowledge are everywhere in America. The university, the computer, and the space-bound satellite all point to the remarkable advances in American technology. Yet men have not found peace, and the world stands on the brink of imminent destruction. Where is the problem? Could the answer to our dilemma be found in our ignorance of the wisdom of God? With all the acquisition of knowledge, we have neglected the proverbs of Israel's ancient wise men.

The Old Testament gives us the Law. Only in the keeping of the Law can a society emerge from the wilderness of man's sin. The Old Testament gives us the Prophets. Through the thunderous pronouncements of the prophets, we learn the tragic consequences that await the man or nation that dares to violate the Law of God.

The Old Testament also gives us the wisdom of God. Job, Proverbs, Ecclesiastes, Song of Solomon, and certain psalms formed for Israel the wisdom writings. In the international arena of wisdom, the wisdom literature of the Old Testament is unique. It alone teaches that wisdom began in a right relationship with the God of love who personally cares for His children.

An Invitation to Wisdom

The Proverbs reflect the depth of insight into the character of God's wisdom given to Solomon after God said to him, "Ask what I shall give thee. Solomon responded, "Give therefore Thy servant an understanding heart to judge Thy people, that I may discern between good and bad.... And the speech pleased the Lord" (1 Kings 3:5-10). Perhaps it would be well to ask, as we begin this study of Proverbs, if we have a deep desire for the wisdom of God.

Solomon recognized, as he penned the Proverbs, that three types of persons would read his words: the fool, the simple, and the scorner. Perhaps even you too will feel the sting of God's reproof as we journey together through this great book that points the way to success in life. If you do find the Lord speaking to you, then whatever He says to you, do it.

Not only did God commend Solomon for his request, but He did more for Solomon than Solomon had ever dreamed He would: "Behold, I have done according to thy words: lo, I have given thee a wise and understanding heart, so that there was none like thee before thee, neither after thee shall any arise like unto thee. And I have also given thee that which thou has not asked, both riches, and honor, so that there shall not be any among the kings like unto thee all thy days" (1 Kings 3:12-13).

God wants to do the same for you. Delight yourself in Him, and He shall give you the desires of your heart (Ps. 37:4). Yes, He is even the God who can do abundantly above all we ask or think (Eph. 3:20).

As we read the description of wisdom in Proverbs 8:22-31, we cannot escape the clear teaching that Jesus Christ is the incarnation of the wisdom of God. "Christ Jesus...," according to the Apostle Paul, "is made unto us wisdom, and righteousness, and sanctification, and redemption: that, according as it is written, He that glorieth, let him glory in the Lord" (1 Cor. 1:30-31).

To yield our lives to Jesus Christ is the ultimate act of wisdom. To be in Him is to be in the wisdom of God. As you contemplate God's wisdom, plan to get into fellowship with God and purpose to live there. Practically, the wisdom of Proverbs can help you get into the will of God and stay there for all your life.

Finding Success

True success is finding the will of God early and living in it throughout life. The will of God may carry you into deprivation or popularity. It may mean America or Africa. Success has nothing to do with position or geography. Success and security are found only in the center of the will of God.

The one who wrote most of the Proverbs should be heard carefully. First, he is Solomon. During his reign, Israel enjoyed a security and a material plenty such as she had never dreamed of and would never know again. This evaluation was due to the great leadership of God's wisest man.

Second, Solomon was the son of David, who was the man after God's own heart. David knew his moments of sin and failure, but he left his son a lasting heritage. David taught his son the ways of God. David was faithful to Deuteronomy 6:7, which instructs the teaching of God's commandments "diligently unto thy children."

The Way of Wisdom

Solomon follows in the steps of his father and instructs the young of his nation in the way of wisdom. Notice Proverbs 1:2-3, "To know wisdom and instruction; to perceive the words of understanding; to receive the instuction of wisdom, justice, and judgment, and equity." Solomon was saying that he was giving his people these proverbs so they might know wisdom. Throughout the Book of Proverbs, we come across the word *wisdom*. The biblical definition of *wisdom,* in a simple fashion, is this: "Seeing all things from God's point of view."

The unredeemed person never sees things from God's point of view. He always views things from an earthly perspective. He is captured by the cosmos. He is imprisoned by the planet on which he lives. His gods are labeled "hedonism" and "immorality," and they are all he worships. We have read again and again of the tragic deaths of actors and actresses. These pathetic figures have worshiped before a false altar of success, and have, in the end, reaped a fatal harvest. The greater catastrophe is that millions who do not enjoy a celebrity's level of prosperity still reject the Word and wisdom of God, and move through life devoid of wisdom, security, and success.

We who have known Christ are seated with Him in the heavenlies (see Eph. 2:6). We can have God's perspective. We can see things from God's point of view.

Solomon states that we who walk with wisdom will also receive instruction. In addition to God's point of view, we need instruction on how to apply that wisdom. The Proverbs provide an abundance of that instruction.

If we would be good leaders, fathers, mothers, businessmen, and businesswomen, we too will spend time with the Proverbs and teach others to do the same. My friend Art DeMoss, who was an insurance executive and is now in heaven, read one chapter from the Book of Proverbs each day. Though I do not follow that practice as closely as Art DeMoss did, I often read Proverbs, and I always discover principles that help me with the problems I am facing.

You can never know true wisdom until you are regenerated by the Spirit of God and indwelt by that One who is the wisdom of God, Jesus Christ. Wisdom is found in the Word of God. Paul told Timothy, "The Holy Scriptures . . . are able to make thee wise" (2 Tim. 3:15). The Scriptures are "profitable for doctrine, for reproof, for correction, for instruction in righteousness; that the man of God may be perfect [complete], throughly furnished unto all good works (2 Tim. 3:16-17). Instruction is the companion of wisdom. The term *instruction* implies a discipline of mind and heart that enables a man to keep himself under control. A man under control, walking in the path of wisdom, is a potent force for good under the hand of God.

This disciplined involvement with wisdom produces a perceptive spirit in a person. Solomon desired that men and women know the Proverbs, for such knowledge enables them to sort out and interpret the issues of life. In Hebrews we encounter the same idea. "Strong meat belongeth to them that are of full age, even those who by reason of use have their senses exercised to discern both good and evil" (Heb. 5:14). Perception—the ability to sort things out properly—belongs only to those who have companioned with wisdom in a disciplined fashion. Such companioning alone allows for the instruction that will, in the long run, produce a perceptive mind.

In verses 2 and 3, we meet other character traits of the person who keeps company with wisdom. Perception and reception are dynamically linked. To openly and continuously receive the instruction of wisdom is to grow in perception. This ability to discern is given only to those who consistently involve themselves with the Word of God (Heb. 4:12) or, in this case, the Proverbs.

Everybody is talking about justice today. The American Civil Liberties Union is constantly talking about justice. But biblical justice is a justice of another kind, introducing another dimension to our conversations on justice. That which is truly just is that which is fitting or right according to the Supreme Judge.

The man of wisdom is a man who wrestles with issues. He discriminates between right and wrong. His discrimination is based on an authoritative standard, the Word of God. When he is convinced that the actions of his leaders or peers are in violation of God's standards, he cannot keep silent. Like the prophets of old, he must speak of God's judgment when a nation violates the principles of justice and equity.

This concern for justice and equity has led thousands of committed Christians to speak out on moral issues in our day. There are those who would say that the people of God should stay out of moral or political issues. They get infuriated when we speak against abortion, pornography, and other moral cancers that threaten to erode the very foundation of America. The man of wisdom will always enter into judgment with a society where the principles of justice and equity are violated.

Receiving Knowledge

In verse 4 we are told of wisdom's benefit to the simple: "To give subtlety to the simple, to the young man knowledge and discretion." The simple are those who are open to good impression but are easily led astray. To these, wisdom will bring subtlety, or the ability to seize opportunities for the good. Men and women often are uncertain about where to apply their efforts. The young are particularly vexed by this uncertainty. Should I go to college, enter the Army, or take a job in a factory? The person who companions with wisdom will enjoy the dividend of wisdom's direction in seizing the right opportunity for the good of himself and all who are involved with him.

To have knowledge is to be in possession of a vast storehouse of facts. Discretion is the possession of an inward sense that allows a man to use those facts in the best possible way. To possess knowledge is one thing, but to possess the discretion that leads to the path of truth and profit is quite another matter. Solomon said, "If the iron be blunt, and he does not whet the edge, then must he put to more strength; but wisdom is profitable to direct" (Ecc. 10:10). What a pathetic picture Solomon draws for us in that text. Here is a person who possesses all of the materials necessary to do a good job of cutting wood in the forest. However, the ax is dull, and the workman will need to work all the harder to cut the wood and will wear himself out in a short time. Discretion mandates that the ax be sharpened before tackling the tasks of life. The sharpness that the combination of knowledge and discretion bring to a man will make him a servant of worth to the Lord. The possession of knowledge alone cannot produce that effective tool.

The intention of the author has been clearly stated. He believes that only through an encounter with the wisdom of God will a person be put on the path to success. Men will miss that point if they do not learn to listen. The New Testament admonishes, "Wherefore, my beloved brethren, let every man be swift to hear, slow to speak, slow to wrath" (James 1:19). When wisdom enters into a man, he will find that he speaks less and listens more. The maturity of a man may often be weighed by noting the time he spends in speaking. One thing is certain, while we are speaking we are not learning.

Proverbs 1:8 reminds the young that they are not only to hear the Lord; they must hear their parents also: "My son, hear the instruction of thy father, and forsake not the law of thy mother." I have been looking at a news article concerning a Baptist pastor in the Soviet Union who has been sentenced to five years of hard labor for teaching Christian principles to his children. This man's property was confiscated, and his fifteen-year-old son was placed in a boarding school, where he is forbidden to have a Bible or pray. Thank God for a country where we have religious freedom. Parents must walk in wisdom, and children must listen to the Lord and their parents.

Solomon tells us who we should not listen to: "My son, if sinners entice thee, consent thou not" (Prov. 1:10). If lawbreakers invite you to join them, tell them you want nothing to do with them. I am amazed that men of high rank will violate the law. ABSCAM senators tried to excuse their behavior. When someone offers you a bribe, get the person's name and turn him in to the police. When leaders begin to compromise their integrity and morality, they have no right to expect anyone to follow them. Don't be enticed by the crooks, the drug pushers, the punk rockers. Learn to follow the path of wisdom to success—"that thou mayest walk in the way of good men, and keep the paths of the righteous" (Prov. 2:20).

"They hated knowledge, and did not choose the fear of the Lord" (Prov. 1:29). We will never become involved in asking or increasing our understanding if we do not first fear the Lord. To many it is unthinkable that we who are in Christ should fear the Lord. Yet again and again we are admonished that "the fear of the Lord is the beginning of wisdom" (Ps. 111:10).

Electricity is an awesome power. When it leaps across the sky on a stormy night, it evokes a variety of responses from observers. Most would indicate a touch of fear as a mighty lightning bolt leaps from the sky and reaches to the earth. While the electricity that courses through wires in our homes is the source of many blessings for us, the sight of a storm-broken bare wire spitting fire into the sky as it convulses along the ground, produces again that sense of fear that is at once constructive and alarming.

The principle seems simple enough. Electricity, when it is channeled through proper means and respected for the great power it possesses, can be a source of great enrichment. Violate those principles once and you will, at best, receive an awesome jolt, at worst, die, with your body broken under the judgment of a tremendous power whose negative possibilities you refused to honor.

Respect and fear lay at the very beginning of our involvement with God's power. It does little good to say, "Later, I will fear it," for later may be too late. All men must bow to God's great power. This is the beginning of wisdom and the beginning of life. Fools are self-willed, headstrong sons who will not heed advice. They can look only for judgment and fiery indignation.

Many in our day object to such a picture of God. We applaud His love—and that we ought to do with even louder applause as we wait for the coming of His Son. However, we do Him a tragic injustice when we do not also cover our faces like the seraphim (Isa. 6:2) and confess His holiness and awesome power. If we err in our time, it is in our refusal to see Him as the all-powerful God. In our thinking we can violate His principles and receive only a slap on the hand. This is not the man of wisdom. To behave in such a way is to work with a dull ax and set ourselves in the way of His chastening rather than in the way of His blessing.

2

Man's Responsibility and God's Provision

Proverbs 2—4

I was eighteen years old when I became a Christian. My only regret is that I wasn't eight instead of eighteen. I am thankful that the Bible tells us not only how to become a Christian but also how to live after we do. The Book of Proverbs is the most concise blueprint for successful living to be found in the sixty-six books of the Bible.

Ten Verbs of Responsibility

In the first five verses of Proverbs 2, we have what I call the Christian's ten verbs of action. You remember from your days in English class that a verb usually denotes action. These ten verbs contain a summary of our responsibility before God. They must be understood and acted on if we are to enjoy the good things that God has for His children.

● The first verb is *receive* (v. 1). We must receive God's Word. Every Sunday I preach to thousands at Thomas Road Baptist Church and to millions over the airwaves. Some who listen receive the Word, but many do not. Some fail to receive because they are preoccupied with what happened yesterday. Some fail to receive because they don't believe the Bible is really worth listening to.

We are told in Acts 2:41 what happens when people receive the Word of God. When Peter preached a great sermon on the Day of Pentecost, "they that gladly received his word were baptized." Receiving the Word of God always brings change. People who believed Peter's words about the death, burial, and resurrection of Jesus Christ were baptized and were added to the church. They made radical changes in their lifestyles.

● The second verb, also in verse 1, admonishes us to *hide* the Lord's commandments in our hearts. The psalmist also reminds us that we are to hide the Word of God in our hearts that we might not sin against the Lord (Ps. 119:11). Solomon is telling us here that we need to memorize the Word of God. Recently, I was talking with some old college friends. Chatting about what was most profitable to us when we were in Bible college, we all agreed that our memory work—hiding the Word of God in our minds—was one of the most important things we did. I wish I could memorize as easily today as I was able to twenty-five years ago. We all ought to memorize Scripture and hide it away so that God can bring it to remembrance when we need it in practical everyday life.

In a Midwestern city not long ago, the twelve-year-old daughter of a prominent surgeon lay seemingly at the point of death, the victim of an apparent virus that had attacked her brain. Lapsing in and out of consciousness, she could be heard reciting Scripture verses that she had learned in Sunday School and in a midweek youth program. What an encouragement to her parents! In time she began to recover and today is a radiant Christian teenager.

● The third verb tells us to *incline* our ears to wisdom (v. 2). *Incline* means to "lean toward." I can often look into the faces of the people I am preaching to and tell whether they are really with it. They are often leaning toward me, and once in a while they even say, "Amen." The Bible is the Word of God, whether you agree with it or not; but when you *incline* your heart toward it, you get the real benefit of its blessing in your life.

● The fourth verb, also in verse 2, tells us to *apply* our hearts to understanding. Without application, the other three verbs are worthless. To receive the Word of God, to memorize Scripture, and to lean toward it are all good. However, we must move on to apply the truths of God's Word to the issues of life.

Consider, for instance, the issues of abortion and homosexuality. When it comes to applying God's Word and taking a stand on these issues, many people back away. They say, "I believe in personal choice." I believe in choice too. But choices should be made on the basis of what the Bible teaches. Irresponsible sexual involvement is the result of not applying God's Word to the sexual area of our lives. When we obey the Word of God and trust Christ as Saviour and Lord, old things pass away and all things become new (see 2 Cor. 5:17). That is application.

● Verb number 5 raises the issue of the intensity with which we seek knowledge. Solomon states that we should *cry* after knowledge (v. 3). The verb *cry* implies to hunger, thirst, or long after. We need to hunger for more and more of the knowledge of God that comes through His Word. I think Solomon has prayer in mind here also. We verbalize a prayer and cry out to God because we hunger for spiritual growth.

● Verb 6 is an intensification of the verb *cry*. We *lift* up our voices for understanding (v. 3). We pour out intercession, supplication, and praise to the Lord.

● Verbs 7 and 8—*seek* and *search*—in verse 4 symbolically portray wisdom as silver and other treasure. This passage speaks again of an attitude of heart. Imagine what would happen if it were announced that there was $1 million in silver or gold buried under the main street of your town. The street would be destroyed in the feverish search for those precious elements.

Do we go after the Word of God in the same way? The Word of God should be so exciting to us that we wear it out. We find a nugget here and there. God will continuously enrich us by giving us treasures from His Word if we approach the Word with expectancy and spiritual hunger. There is nothing monotonous about the Christian life. Out of His bountiful treasury, God gives us something new and valuable every day.

● "Then shalt thou *understand*" (v. 9). That is the ninth verb. As we begin to grow in the grace and knowledge of the Lord, we develop spiritual understanding. The outcome of this understanding is fear of the Lord. Not many people fear the Lord today. If people feared God, you couldn't get doctors to perform abortions; you couldn't get printers to print pornography, and drug pushers would quit in a day. There will come a day when they all will meet God. Fear will cover them like a garment as they are transported to hell for all eternity.

● The tenth and final verb is *find*. As we study God's Word, we will *find* the knowledge of God (v. 5). We do not accidentally stumble on a good relationship with the Lord. There are no easy shortcuts to holiness. We cannot line people up, shout and scream, and zap holiness into them. It just does not work that way in life. We have to work at growing in practical holiness every day. We must work out our own salvation with fear and trembling. This has nothing to do with going to heaven. It has to do with becoming like Jesus while we are making the journey: "For the Lord giveth wisdom; out of His mouth cometh knowledge and understanding" (2:6).

God's Five Verbs

You have seen ten verbs of action. They tell us what we must do if we are going to be successful. Now let's look at five verbs that tell us what the Lord is going to do for us. I have said that wisdom is "seeing things from God's point of view." How do we acquire that kind of wisdom?

● God gives or imparts wisdom. How do birds know when it is time to go south in the winter and north in the summer? God has imparted that understanding to them. God *gives* wisdom. We do not need to have an annual nervous breakdown. If we need wisdom, we can ask of God and He will give it to us (see James 1:5).

● The second verb signifies God's wealth of knowledge and understanding: "Out of His mouth *cometh* knowledge and understanding" (v. 6). The best-educated person in the world is an intellectual midget beside the Lord. The wisest person is the person who recognizes his responsibility to get his marching orders from the Word of God.

● The third verb is in verse 7. Solomon tells us that God "*layeth* up sound wisdom for the righteous." God is stacking up wisdom for us. He is building us a reservoir of spiritual traits and characteristics. He intends that His people drink deeply from that reservoir.

● God also *keeps* the path of judgment (v. 8). *Keeps* is the fourth verb. God is our protector. God's man is indestructible until he has finished the work God has given him to do. We do not have to be afraid of death. I have a friend who often talks about death. If he has a pain, he's sure it's cancer. I never think about death. I know I am going to die. I have made preparation for the journey. God is my shield. He takes care of me and He takes care of you.

● "He . . . *preserveth* the way of His saints" (v. 8). *Preserve* is the fifth verb telling what God will do for us. God intends to finish what He has started. He is our preserver. Whenever I autograph a Bible, I always write Philippians 1:6 under my name. It says that we can be confident that He who has begun a good work in us will perform it, or finish it, until the day of Jesus Christ. God always finishes what He starts.

We have ten verbs of action relating to our responsibility before the Lord. We have seen God's response. He gives us five things. When these fifteen verbs are in action, what happens? "Then shalt thou understand righteousness, and judgment, and equity; yea, every good path" (Prov. 2:9).

These fifteen verbs promise that God will let us know when we are doing wrong and will encourage us when we are doing right. They promise that when we are obedient we will have three things:

- righteousness, or the ability to live
- judgment, or the ability to discern our way through the thorny problems of life
- equity, or the ability to give everyone a fair deal

The end result of implementing these fifteen verbs in our experience is that we will be spared from two disastrous lifestyles—the way of "the evil man" (v. 12) and the plague of "the strange woman" (v. 16). She is representative of immorality. God wants to deliver His people from all that is dishonest and from sexual immorality.

Obedience and Trust Bring Blessings

In Proverbs 3, Solomon reminds: "My son, forget not my law; but let thine heart keep my commandments; for length of days, and long life, and peace, shall they add to thee" (vv. 1-2).

After we have loved the Lord, served Him, and been used by God, we may forget His commandments and forfeit all of the blessings and privileges that come through obedience. We won't lose our salvation, but we will lose our joy. People who love the Lord and keep His commandments are happier and they live longer. Any insurance man can verify that averages show that Christians, who keep God's laws and do not use tobacco, alcohol, and drugs, live longer than many others. If there were not other reasons for serving God than the temporal, you ought to serve God.

Solomon goes on to say in verses 4-10 that obedience to the Word of God will not only bring physical blessing, but it will also bring good success in the sight of God and man. Be sure to measure your success under the careful standards of God's watchful eye. People usually measure success by what a person has gathered materially. This is not valid by divine standards. There are people who will never get in the headlines, yet God views them as successful. They are obedient and dependable. They are available to the Lord, and their lives are pure and clean.

"Trust in the Lord with all thine heart; and lean not unto thine own understanding. In all thy ways acknowledge Him, and He shall direct thy paths" (vv. 5-6). Here we have two of the most popular verses in the Bible. Many have made these their life verses. If we understand nothing from Proverbs but the content of these verses, our study of the book will be worth it. Here is where most of us fall down spiritually and lose our birthright. We fail to trust in the Lord with all our heart.

Why do we worry? Why do we scheme? Why do some of us have our annual nervous breakdown? I think the basic problem is that we have not yet learned to trust the Lord. We cannot trust the Lord unless we know what He has said. That means we need to know what the Bible has to say. We must each be a Bible reader, believer, obeyer, and memorizer. We must make the Word of God the delight of our heart. This internalizing of God's Word will open the way to trust.

We look to the Lord for all of our needs. When we trust Him with all of our heart, we do not let go. If the need is not immediately met, we just go back to Him, trust in Him, and lean on Him more. In His time and on His schedule, He will provide that need. He supplies all our needs through Christ Jesus.

The problem we often encounter is contained in the next phrase. We are exhorted to "lean not unto [our] own understanding." We often try with our own intellect to chart the course that we want God to sanctify in our lives and work. Someone has said that living by faith is living without scheming. Most of us are schemers. We are like Jacob before his wrestling match with the Lord. God has to break us and sometimes cripple us to get us to stop scheming and start trusting.

This does not mean that you do not use the intellect God has given you. It means that when you are totally leaning on the Lord and trusting Him, logic and analysis may not always work. God wants to do something that has not been done before. He wants to work in a way that He has never worked before in your life.

If we ever want to experience His work in this manner in our lives, we must trust Him and acknowledge Him. We acknowledge the Lord in church. Our prayers, hymns, and meditation on God's Word in our church services acknowledge Him. Most believers acknowledge Him by saying grace before meals. We need to acknowledge Him in our business life, our social life, our dating life, and our educational life. Too often God is just someone we call into the foxhole when things are really getting rough. We need to acknowledge Him in every area of life.

When we lean on the Lord and live by faith, there is never a problem with pride. We recognize that God alone is keeping us afloat, that He is supplying us the wisdom to live by. We know that He is providing our needs at every turn. He alone gives us health and strength. He keeps our hearts pumping blood. How could we ever, then, be wise in our own eyes?

Verse 8 reiterates what is stated in verse 2. Trusting and fearing the Lord is the foundation of health. I am convinced that there are many illnesses in our society that result from spiritual breakdown. When you are spiritually broken down, your body is affected. When a man's heart is on fire for God, when he is filled with love, when there is no hate or malice in him, he has more strength. If you will follow Scripture, it shall be health to your body and marrow to your bones (v. 8).

Honor the Lord

The first key word in Proverbs 3 is *trust* (v. 5). The second key word is *honor:* "Honor the Lord with thy substance, and with the firstfruits of all thine increase" (v. 9). We are to honor the Lord. We can honor the Lord by taking our substance and putting it all in His hands. Do you wonder why God has blessed you the way He has? Why He has given you your needs and more? He has done so because He loves you and He is honoring you. That honor must be returned. We preach tithes and offerings at Thomas Road. I believe that every Christian—by both Old and New Testament mandate—has an obligation to give God a minimum of the first tenth of his total income. That is not all that belongs to God. In reality, everything that we own belongs to the Lord. We who are under grace should give the Lord at least as much as the Jews had to give under the Law. We should just begin there.

God not only honors His people, He also chastens them. In verse 11, we are encouraged never to despise the chastening of the Lord. When you find a bitter Christian, he is not really bitter against his circumstances, he is bitter against the Lord who allowed his circumstances. Most people will not say, "I'm mad at God." They do not want to put on the gloves with God. Our arms are too short to box with God. Hence, most people say they are bitter with their circumstances.

Solomon affirms that our circumstances really are used by God as instruments for our maturing (vv. 11-12). We ought not to weary of the Lord's correction. It is an evidence of His love for us. You and I are going through a correction process constantly. It is all necessary—a part of growing up, a part of life. The Lord continuously polishes His shafts.

Four Ps of Proverbs 3

"Happy is the man that findeth wisdom, and the man that getteth understanding" (v. 13). Verses 13-19 constitute the second division of chapter 3. I have broken this portion into several sections. Each section can be represented by a *P*.

● *Profit*—Verse 14 informs us that there is real spiritual profit in getting divine wisdom. Learning to see things from God's point of view puts a man on the path to profit.

● *Precious*—Verse 15 tells us that wisdom is of great value. She is more precious than rubies. That is why I would challenge you to get God's wisdom into your mind.

● *Pleasantness and peace*—These *Ps* are found in verse 17: "Her ways are ways of pleasantness, and all her paths are peace." God does not want His people in turmoil all the time. Some people make me nervous. I can tell there is fire burning inside them; they are angry and have no inward peace. God's peace keeps us in the eye of the storm and releases us from the fear of destruction. We do not have to live with fear and agitation, because wisdom and understanding are a tree of life to us.

"The Lord by wisdom hath founded the earth" (v. 19). This wisdom that God used in creating the world is the wisdom He makes available to us. I was amused to read in our local newspaper about a conflict between two evolutionists at a nearby college. They could not agree on the age of the earth or how the missing link came into the picture. How wonderful to know with David, Abraham, Solomon, and a host of others that the Lord created all things. He spoke the world into existence and is wise enough to name and number everything in it.

He made everything; He owns everything. By His knowledge the depths are broken up. The springs, the rivers, all that is under the earth, the clouds above, the rain falling from the sky have been created by His wisdom. If we consistently tap into that wisdom, God will enable us to live longer, healthier, more pleasant and peaceful lives.

"My son, let not them depart from thine eyes: keep sound wisdom and discretion" (v. 21). These are exciting words. So many people are not living life; they are just enduring. I have never seen so many people in trouble. Lives are falling apart. Homes are falling apart. Are you really living life? Bearing up under all the burdens and seeing all the evil today is tough— but God gives grace. He never gives us more than we can bear (2 Cor. 10:13). He always gives wisdom to those who ask for it (James 1:5).

Pay Your Debts
In concluding chapter 3, Solomon reminds the recipients of divine wisdom that they ought never to withhold "good from them to whom it is due" (v. 27). This is another way of saying, "Pay your honest debts." When you have difficulty meeting your obligations, go to the people you owe and explain your situation. Explain that you have no intention of defrauding them. Stay in touch with creditors. Keep the lines of communication open and, as soon as you are able, pay the debt. Bankruptcy laws are being abused today. They were never intended to help people get out of paying their debts but rather to give relief so they could pay their debts.

Our ministry here in Lynchburg is now twenty-eight years old. We have had hard times. We have had to trust God one day at a time. There have been instances when we have had to ask our creditors for an extension. They know we pay our debts. If a man is honest, he will pay you somehow, sometime, someway.

The curse of God is on the man of violence, but the blessing of the Lord is on that man who trusts God and lives peacefully. God wants us to use things and love people. He is opposed to the man who loves *things* and uses *people.* God wants us to be fair with everyone with whom we come in contact in our daily walk and talk. Here is how Paul said it to the Ephesians: "Be ye kind one to another, tenderhearted, forgiving one another, even as God for Christ's sake hath forgiven you" (4:32).

That is the Christian life. That is the life that Jesus lived. Jesus was no sissy. He was firm. He was stable. He was a man. He was also *LOVE.* He never misused or hurt anyone. Even in His dying words He spoke of forgiveness. If we cannot trust God to take care of us against those who would attempt to do us in, then whom shall we turn to? He will surely scorn the scorners and give grace to the humble.

Parents and Children

The burden of chapter 4 is the child. It begins, "Hear, ye children, the instruction of a father, and attend to know understanding." Young people who would be successful in life must learn to hear their parents. The other side of the coin is that parents have an awesome responsibility. Parents must teach children the truths of God's Word. The home, the church, and the Christian school form the tripod on which children's Christian character development must stand.

The father's responsibility to instruct his son is the focus here. We thank God for mother, but biblically the father is responsible for leading the family spiritually. He needs to teach his children sound doctrine.

Spiritual decline comes when children move away from

the biblical direction implanted by the parents. Solomon enjoins the young people of Israel to retain the words of their fathers in their hearts. In verse 6 he pleads with them not to forsake wisdom. Wisdom is "the mainest thing," as I have heard young people say. Get the divine perspective on everything, and you will be successful.

With wisdom we want also to gain understanding. We need to understand why we do what we do, and do not do what we should. Most of my conduct is governed by the reality that I have only one life and I want to glorify God with it. I do not want to ruin my influence by doing things that dishonor Christ.

Notice in verse 10 that when we receive the sayings of wisdom, our years will be many. This is one of the side effects of living for God. That does not mean that you are out of the will of God if you are sick. God has a greater purpose that He often accomplishes through suffering. However, when you look at the total picture, I believe those who live by God's principles live better and live longer.

"Go not in the way of evil men" (v. 14). Do not make bad associations. Rather, keep God's words as faithful companions in the midst of your heart. This whole matter of godliness starts with the heart. You are on the way when the Word of God dwells within your heart. That is where it starts. Notice, however, that it does not end there. Soon the mouth is involved (v. 24), then the eyes (v. 25), and finally the feet (v. 26).

Let us commit ourselves afresh today to the Spirit of God and trust Him to keep us from going to the right or the left (v. 27). Let us trust Him and work with Him to keep ourselves right on course.

3

How to Live Successfully

Proverbs 5—7

President Woodrow Wilson once expressed some thoughts on success that run parallel to a biblical concept. He said, "I would rather fail in a cause that someday will triumph than triumph in a cause that someday will fail." We must be on God's side for success to have any meaning at all. Supposed success outside of God's program is in reality just failure.

All thirty-one chapters of Proverbs tell how to live successfully. The theme of chapter 5 is biblical morality, or how to succeed in the moral arena.

Situation Ethics Rules

We are living in a world today that knows very little about morality. We have in our nation a real effort to secularize, to literally throw God out of society, and to adopt situation ethics instead of the traditional Judeo-Christian ethics as our behavior code. What is situation ethics? It is basically "anything is right under the right circumstances." Nothing is ever absolutely wrong. There are no absolute codes to tell men and women how they should live. In other words, circumstances dictate how we should act and react in each situation. In the Book of Judges, during that bloody and violent time in the history of the nation of Israel, we are told that "in those days there was no king," no authority, no absolute ethic, and "every man did that which was right in his own eyes" (Jud. 17:6; 21:25). That is nothing but anarchy.

Society is becoming increasingly opposed to any biblical standards of righteousness. Some organizations today are dedicated to throwing God out of society, forbidding prayer in public buildings, and banning the use of chaplains in Congress and in the armed services. Their goals are based on the false, hypocritical premise that it is unconstitutional to impose religious views on the public. But our Founding Fathers, who did believe in separation of church and state, did not believe in separation of God and state. That is why, to the present day, Congress and the Supreme Court open their sessions with prayer. And upon the walls of many buildings in our nation's capital are verses of Scripture and many inscriptions that indicate our Founding Fathers' faith in God.

Shun the "Strange Woman"

Solomon, under divine inspiration, is saying to sons and daughters today: "My son, attend unto my wisdom, and bow thine ear to my understanding, that thou mayest regard discretion [that is, good judgment], and that thy lips may keep knowledge. For the lips of a strange woman drop as an honeycomb, and her mouth is smoother than oil, but her end [i.e., her goal] is bitter as wormwood, sharp as a two-edged sword. Her feet go down to death; her steps take hold on hell" (Prov. 5:1-5). Here is God's instruction through Solomon to the sons and the daughters of this and every generation: "One man for one woman, for one lifetime." Here is God saying to the young man, "Do not be enticed by loose women. Do not think you can have premarital sex, or extramarital sex, and not suffer the consequences."

I am fully aware of the peer pressure on young people today. In the youth society of our day, the drug culture, the music scene, the television and movie industries, and the publishing industry, great pressure is directed toward getting young people involved in illicit sex as early as possible. But let me take you to Solomon, the wisest man who ever lived, who 3,500 years ago said, "The lips of a strange woman drop as an honeycomb . . . but her end is bitter as wormwood . . . her feet go down to death; her steps take hold on hell." We have here the rules and regulations for successful living. Your body belongs to God, and you need to keep it pure.

As the chancellor of Liberty Baptist College and Seminary, I can testify that in the thirteen years of the existence of our schools, now with over 6,000 students, every year it is a little tougher. That is because the students coming here each year are a little more permissive than the year before. They have not gone bad. But Mom and Dad are not taking the same biblical stand they once did. Many schools and churches are not taking a stand. Educators and social engineers are too often on the wrong side. We need to heed Solomon's warning on moral purity.

There is a God in heaven who says illicit sex is wrong, abortion is wrong, homosexuality is wrong. There is a God in heaven who says, "Whatsoever a man soweth, that shall he also reap" (Gal. 6:7). There is a God in heaven who says, "Be sure your sin will find you out" (Num. 32:23). And Solomon is telling us to stay away from immorality (Prov. 5:7): "Hear me now therefore, O ye children, and depart not from the words of my mouth." That is a command. Listen! Do not depart from it. The time has come for preachers and Christian parents to teach our children what is right and wrong. Solomon did that a long, long time ago.

In Proverbs 5:8 he said, "Remove thy way far from her, and

come not nigh the door of her house." Stay away from immorality "lest thou give thine honor unto others, and thy years unto the cruel" (v. 9). What is going to happen if you do not stay away? You are going to lose your testimony. You are going to lose your self-respect, and you are going to lose years off your life. Verse 10 says that something else will happen to you: "Strangers [will] be filled with thy wealth." You will lose your money. If you have no other reason for living a moral life than a mercenary one, that is a good one, because you will lose your money if you live immorally. "And thy labors be in the house of a stranger" (v. 10). Somebody else will benefit from what you have done.

How many people do you know who have lost their businesses, their homes, their families, even their jobs because of immorality? Hear Solomon declare the truth: "Lest strangers be filled with thy wealth; and thy labors be in the house of a stranger; and thou mourn at the last, when thy flesh and thy body are consumed" (vv. 10-12). That describes venereal diseases, which are at epidemic proportions in this country. They are literally destroying bodies and minds. Could anything be worth the price one pays for going against the biblical standards of morality? I think not. For those who trample God's laws, the time will come when they will pay the price with their bodies, homes, families, and self-respect. They will abbreviate their lives and lose everybody in the world who is precious to them.

Verse 12 goes on to point out that those who despise God's laws will finally say, "How have I hated instruction." "Why wouldn't I listen?" This is what the adulterer will say in the end when it is too late. "Why did I not listen in my heart?" "My heart despised reproof." "I would not let anybody tell me anything." "[I] have not obeyed the voice of my teachers, nor inclined mine ear to them that instructed me!" (v. 13) Television has contributed to this attitude. The publishing industry, the public schools, and the movie industry have done their part. But I think pastors who do not have the backbone to stand up and say what needs to be said have done their part too.

Verse 15 contains advice for husbands: "Drink waters out of thine own cistern, and running waters out of thine own well." Do you know what that means? A husband and wife are to receive total sexual pleasure only with each other. "Let her breasts satisfy thee at all times, and be thou ravished [exhilarated] always with her love. And why wilt thou, my son, be ravished with a strange woman, and embrace the bosom of a stranger?" (vv. 19-20) Listen: "For the ways of man are before the eyes of the Lord" (v. 21). God Almighty is looking on. He is writing it all down, and at the Judgment Bar all who sin are going to face every bit of it. And they will pay the price between now and then: "For the ways of man are before the eyes of the Lord, and He pondereth all his goings. His own iniquities shall take the wicked himself, and he shall be holden with the cords of his sins. He shall die without instruction, and in the greatness of his folly he shall go astray" (vv. 21-23).

We can help change the direction of society by living a morally pure life and by God's help seeing to it that our children and grandchildren grow up in a society different from that which the liberals are trying to create.

Seven Things God Hates
You will find the heart of Proverbs 6 in verses 16-19, where Solomon says there are seven things God hates. He enumerates them.

● First, God hates "a proud look" (v. 17). Pride goes before destruction. And when God finds pride or a proud look in us, He must bring us down before He can use us.

● Second, God hates "a lying tongue" (v. 17). God is

against dishonesty. We live in a world today wrapped in dishonesty. It seems that contracts mean nothing; man's word means little. When we read the media today, we are seldom certain how much is the truth.

● Third, God hates "hands that shed innocent blood" (v. 17). God hates violence, and our nation today is very close to violence. What is happening in South America, Central America, and the Middle East could very well become the rule and not the exception in this country in this decade. That kind of violence is being spawned from Moscow, and it is being exported all over the world today.

● Then, fourth, there is the "heart that deviseth wicked imaginations" (v. 18)—that is, plots evil. God hates the plotting of evil.

● And, fifth, God hates "feet...swift in running to mischief" (v. 18). God hates the eagerness to do wrong; He wants us to be eager to do right.

● Then, sixth, God despises "a false witness that speaketh lies" (v. 19).

● And, seventh, He hates that one "that soweth discord among brethren" (v. 19). God wants the brethren to love one another.

Recipe for a Wrecked Life
Chapter 6 of Proverbs has four divisions, all giving a clear recipe for a wrecked and ruined life.

● Number 1, violate scriptural principles in economics and make bad financial decisions (vv. 1-5). Solomon begins by saying, "My son, if thou be surety for thy friend, if thou has stricken thy hand with a stranger," and Solomon urges you to run to him and get on your knees and beg him to get out. Now what does that mean? It means that if you have signed or endorsed a note for your friend, go to him and beg to let you off the note. Do whatever you have to do. Verse 4 warns that you should not even sleep till you get out of it, because (v. 5) whether you know it or not, like a little deer you are just waiting for the hunter's arrow to go right through your heart! Like the little bird, the hand of the fowler is about to get you.

You ask, Is it wrong to endorse a note? Not if you can meet three criteria: First, determine in your heart that if you have to pay the note, and you probably will, you will not be mad about it. Conclude in your heart that you are making a gift to this individual. If he or she happens to pay it off, that's a bonus. Second, do not endorse a note if having to pay it off will injure your family in any way. Your first obligation, after God, is to your family, and if endorsing a note is going to injure your family or cause them to suffer loss, you should not do it.

Third, be sure that the Spirit of God leads you to sign it. If you are not fully convinced of all three, then do not sign the note. The first ingredient for a wrecked life is to make bad financial decisions (vv. 1-5).

● The second division of chapter 6 concerns bad work habits (vv. 6-11). This would make a good sermon in America today. Workers talk about three- and four-day work weeks. The "get-all-you-can-and-can-all-you-get" philosophy is not biblical. God says that by the sweat of your brow you will earn your bread. Part of our welfare and unemployment problem is that a lot of people are not looking for jobs. They are looking for positions! Listen to what Solomon is saying in verse 6: "Go to the ant, thou sluggard." Do you know what a sluggard is? The modern translation is "work-hater." Go to the ant, work-hater, and look at her. First of all, she's self-motivated (v. 7). She has no guide, overseer, or ruler. She just gets up on her own, sets her own clock, goes to work, works during the summer in the warmth and the sunshine. Nobody needs to motivate her. Nobody is holding a gun on her. She works because she believes in it. Now, if you are a Christian and are working for somebody, you ought to give him eight good hours a day because you are a Christian.

Not only is the ant self-motivated, but she provides her meat in the summer (v. 8). She's a planner—she prepares ahead of time and she stores up food. She is getting ready for the bad days ahead.

● But if you want to wreck your life, there is a third thing you can do: Have bad character (vv. 12-15). What is a naughty person? That is a wicked person who walks with a froward mouth. First of all, he winks with his eyes, speaks with his feet, teaches with his fingers (v. 13). That means he is dishonest—he is saying one thing with his words, but with his facial expressions and his hands and feet he means something else. And "frowardness is in his heart" (v. 14). He has a rebellious nature; he is dishonest and rebellious.

You will never be a good leader till you learn to be a good follower. Develop a good servant's heart. Learn to say, "Yes, sir" and "No, sir." Learn to obey authority. When you are in the military and are given an order, you don't ask why. You just obey because you are a soldier. You are a military person. You are under authority: pastors, teachers, bosses, moms and dads. We are under authority, and we ought to obey the powers that be. We ought to do it with a right heart attitude, as a matter of developing character.

● Finally, note division 4, verses 20-35: Bad moral behavior will wreck your life. Solomon says, "My son, keep thy father's commandment and forsake not the law of thy mother" (v. 20). Why? Because she told you to stay away from wicked women, to stay out of prostitution, immorality, premarital and extramarital sex (v. 24).

The time has come when we need to take our stand on what is right. If we are going to succeed in life, we must handle our finances properly, have proper work habits, develop proper character, and shun bad moral behavior. If we violate those rules, our lives will go into wreck and ruin. If we will follow those principles, we can be successful in life. That is what Solomon said under divine inspiration. It was true 3,500 years ago, and it is still true today.

Internalizing God's Wisdom

The first seven chapters of Proverbs give advice or counsel of godly parents to their children. In chapter 7, Solomon concludes his remarks to his own children, saying, "My son, keep my words, and lay up my commandments with thee" (v. 1). Then he gives us in order of priority three facts we need to internalize. Number 1, "Keep my commandments, and live; and my law as the apple of thine eye" (v. 2). Keep the Law as the pupil or the most sensitive part of the eye, the most important part of your sight apparatus. Number 1 is the Law. Number 2, "Say unto wisdom, Thou art my sister" (v. 4). Right behind Law is wisdom. The word *wisdom* means "seeing things from God's point of view; seeing things from God's perspective." Let that be very important to you, second only to the keeping of God's Law in your life. And number 3, "Call understanding thy kinswoman" (v. 4) or a close friend.   And in that order of priority, let understanding or knowledge be placed. So here we have it in order of importance in your life. Number 1, obedience to the Law of God. Number 2, wisdom or understanding of what God is doing in your life, in the lives of others, and in history. Number 3, understanding or the constant internalizing and application of knowledge in your head, in your heart, in your life.

All three are progressive actions. We come to know the Law of God by reading the Word of God. How important is it that you read the Bible? How important is it that you know what the Bible has to say? It is as important as the pupil of your eye is to your sight. When some object is hurled toward your face, your eyelid automatically closes instantly in order to protect the pupil of the eye. Thank God for that built-in apparatus. God knew how important the eye is to human beings. So He gave us an eyelid that responds to movement, to any kind of danger, to immediately protect the pupil of the eye. The Law of God is that vital. You are to read the Bible, not so much for the promises but for the commandments. Thank God for the promises—you can claim them every day in your life. But read the Bible primarily for the commandments.

Sometimes when I do not understand what God is doing and do not have the wisdom and understanding to know where God is taking me, in blind obedience I just do what God says. It is amazing how important that is. That is the pupil of the eye. That is what protects me from hurt and from harm. That is what keeps me on the right path doing the right thing. This is where all the libertarian movements are in trouble today.

There are all kinds of libertarian movements today. They talk about freedom of choice. What they mean by *freedom of choice* is freedom of choice to live licentiously; to live immorally; to live in moral permissiveness; and when they get in trouble, to kill the consequences. Abortion is the license to live in a lewd and licentious way without paying the price. It is an attempt by man to circumvent God's law of sowing and reaping. "Whatsoever a man soweth, that shall he also reap" (Gal. 6:7). And the libertarians say, "No, that isn't true, God; we're not going to pay attention to the commandment, 'Thou shalt not kill.' We will kill if we want to. We have a Supreme Court that has made it legal; and therefore, since it is legal, it is right." That is a wrong assumption. Because something is legal does not make it moral. Because something is legal does not mean it is right.

In Proverbs 7:1, Solomon said to keep the Law of God.

People for the American Way and other libertarian groups are saying, in my opinion, "There is no law—do your own thing. If it feels good, do it." That is secular humanism. That is situation ethics, and that is what has gotten the United States in the mess that it is in today. The time has come for Bible preachers and Christians and parents to stand up on their hind legs and say, "The Law of God is pure." Ours is a nation under God, and we should applaud our President when he stands before American people and says, "I've never known a little child who was injured or harmed by being exposed to prayer in a public classroom." He called this a "nation under God," and I agree with him.

In addition to hiding God's law in our hearts, let us get wisdom through prayer and spiritual growth. Let us learn that God has a plan, a will, a work for our lives. As we stay close to God, He will see to it that our lives count for Him.

And, finally, call understanding. Call your "close friend." Do you know why you should read your Bible daily? To increase understanding and knowledge of the Word of God. The best-educated person in America is the person, whoever he is, who best understands the Word of God.

4

Wisdom:
The Key to Life

Proverbs 8—9

Someone has said that the road to success is dotted with many tempting parking places. Satan places his allurements all along the way to make it easy to quit or to get off the track for God. That is why it is so important to find the right road and stay on it.

Solomon has a lot to say about living successfully or living in the will of God as early as possible and for as long as possible. As mentioned earlier, divine wisdom is seeing things from God's perspective, from God's point of view. But how may we know and understand things from God's point of view? Chapter 8 begins by declaring that wisdom is outside crying. Jesus is knocking on the door of our hearts. He wants to come in and be our completeness. He wants to become our life, our strength, our grace, our love. He wants to be everything we need.

Wisdom Wants You

Let's look closer at this thing called wisdom. In the first six verses of chapter 8, wisdom says, "I'm after you. I am chasing you." Did you know that you are not going after God? God is going after you! You are not seeking after the Lord; He is seeking after you. You are the lost sheep. He is the Shepherd, and He has been looking for you and going after you all your life. And now He says wisdom is truth (v. 7). All the truth there is in the universe is in Jesus Christ, our Lord. This old world is so dark, so sinful, so dishonest, and so deceitful. But Jesus Christ is wisdom and speaks the truth.

Look at another thing wisdom does when Jesus lives in your heart: "All the words of my mouth are in righteousness; there is nothing froward [or rebellious] or perverse in them" (v. 8). When Jesus lives in your heart and He is the Lord of your life, you live right. You will not hang out in the old places anymore.

"They are all plain to him that understandeth" (v. 9). That means they are simple. The truths of God are not complicated. A little child can know Jesus and live the Bible way, because God has made the way of life so simple that even a fool need not err in finding it. God's wisdom always makes sense in the long haul. Receive God's instruction and not silver (v. 10). The wisdom of God gives instruction on how to live, the steps to take, the direction to go. Verse 12 says, "I, wisdom, dwell with prudence." The wisdom of God is always tactful and gracious and discerning and has the future in view.

Verse 14 says, "Counsel [advice] is Mine." Do you need advice today? Then if Jesus Christ is in your heart and you know how to pray and how to read His Word, He will provide you the counsel and the direction you need every day to live the Christian life successfully.

I like the last statement in verse 14, "I have strength." Who needs strength? Who feels weak? I am under assault all the time, and so are you. Everybody who names the name of Christ is going upstream against the tide. It isn't possible to live the Christian life on your own; only Jesus Christ living in you can live that Christian life out through you. He is the One who can give you the counsel and the strength to keep on keeping on.

"By Me kings reign, and princes decree justice" (v. 15). God gives administrative ability through Jesus who lives in the believer. God gives that spirit of fairness. Do you know who the fairest people in the world are? People indwelt by the Spirit of the living God, because wisdom decrees justice. They never mistreat anybody. Wisdom belongs to everybody who loves the Lord: "I love them that love Me; and those that seek Me early shall find me" (v. 17).

Christ Provides

The rest of Proverbs 8 tells us that knowing Christ brings all the provisions we need. Verse 18 speaks of "riches and honor" and the last phrase calls it "durable riches." Knowing Christ may not be money in the bank, but it is durable riches, riches that last. Whatever your needs are, your God shall supply them.

"I lead in the way of righteousness" (v. 20). This wisdom, Christ living in us, leads us in the way everlasting. And verse 21 declares, "That I may cause those that love Me to inherit substance, and I will fill their treasures [treasuries]," meaning, "I'll provide their needs. I'll care for their children." Then God goes on to let us know that Christ really is the Lord, because verses 22-27 say that the heavenly Father possessed wisdom in the beginning of His way, and wisdom was set up from everlasting to everlasting. Wisdom [Christ] was there before God created the earth. Verse 28 adds that when He established the clouds, wisdom was there. Wisdom was present when He gave the sea the order not to cover the land (v. 29). Do you know why the waves go just so far up on the land and pull back? Because God gave them a decree and said, "Here's how far you can go." He told the waves and the oceans and the winds, "I am the Lord of Creation." He spoke it into existence. He is the Son of Creation, the Lord of the universe.

Wisdom then goes on to say, "I was by Him [God]. . . . I was daily His delight, rejoicing always before Him, rejoicing in the habitable part of His earth" (vv. 30-31). That means where the people live. Do you know what Jesus is happy about? Not buildings and budgets and programs. The thing that makes Jesus glad is people. He loved people enough to die on a cross to keep them out of hell. And, verse 35, "Whoso findeth Me findeth life [whoever finds Jesus], and shall obtain favor of the Lord." Have you found Jesus yet? Do you know He died for you, rose from the dead for you? Have you invited Him—Wisdom personified, Jesus the Lord—into your heart and life? If not, you need to do so today.

Many Christians once invited Jesus, the Wisdom of God, to save them but later put Him into a corner of their lives. If you are one who has done so, invite Him back up out of the corner and into the center of your life. He is the One you need to guide you. You cannot be successful without His complete leadership in your life.

Wisdom, Man's Greatest Invitation

Proverbs 9 begins with the key word *wisdom.* I have previously defined the word wisdom as "seeing things from God's persepective, seeing things from God's point of view." I also pointed out that God the Father made Jesus to be our wisdom and sanctification and righteousness and redemption (1 Cor. 1:30). Think of it! God has made Jesus, the Saviour, His Son, to be our wisdom! Jesus then lives within us by the Holy Spirit, and Jesus Christ is our wisdom. Strength, holy boldness, courage, love, patience, and so on—all of these are in one person, Jesus Christ.

So Proverbs 9:1 can read this way: "Wisdom has built a palace upon seven pillars." Why seven pillars? Well, seven is the number of God. Seven is the number of perfection, and the house of God is a perfect house. The house of God, that place where you and I will spend eternity, is a perfect place where redeemed people, made perfect in Christ, will spend a perfect eternity. So, in verse 1 we have Jesus, the Lord, who is building a house. That is what He went away to do. He left here nearly 2,000 years ago. He told His disciples, "If I go and prepare a place for you, I will come again, and receive you unto Myself, that where I am, there ye may be also" (John 14:3). He said He was going to prepare a place for us. He is building a house with seven pillars because seven is the number of God.

In Proverbs 9:2-5, Christ is preparing a banquet. Kill that which will provide the meat for the table. Furnish the table (v. 2). The maidens have gone out delivering the invitations, saying, "Come in and eat with Me. Come and dine." And we are told that all may come, no matter who they are or where they are from. Isaiah said that the banquet is free. All who desire may come freely to eat and dine with the Lord (Isa. 55:1-2).

Proverbs 9:4-5 invites those who are simple to come to the banquet—and that includes all of us. "Let him turn in hither; as for him that wanteth understanding, she saith to him, Come, eat of my bread, and drink of the wine which I have mingled." Verse 6 admonishes us to "forsake the foolish, and live; and go in the way of understandng."

What is our Lord Jesus doing today? He is preparing a house, and He is preparing a banquet. Have you ever stopped to think of the Marriage Supper of the Lamb? The Lord Jesus is preparing a banquet unlike anything we have ever seen.

I was with a group invited to dinner at the White House with President Reagan. I do not know how all the others in the room felt, but I know how I felt. I was honored. When the

President walked in, I stood, as did everybody else. When he sat down, we sat down. When he began to eat after the prayer, we began to eat. And we had a wonderful time at his table in the White House. That was a great honor, and I felt privileged just to be there. But have you stopped to think that you and I are going to sit down to a table one day that makes that table at the White House seem like Pete's Diner? That is a fact. When the Lord Jesus walks in, we won't stand. We will all fall on our faces. And after He delivers the invocation and the blessings, we will sit down at the Marriage Supper of the Lamb!

In some of our cities, I speak at banquets hosting a couple of thousand people. I consider that to be a large banquet. But there will be millions at Jesus' banquet. Jesus will be at the table, and we will dine with Him. Why? Because 2,000 years ago, Wisdom—the Lord Jesus Christ—the God-man, Wisdom personified, left heaven. He was born of the Virgin Mary, and tabernacled among men for thirty-three years. He lived a sinless life, died on a cruel cross, and shed His divine blood for my sins and yours. He was buried, rose from the grave on the third day, and now says, "Come and dine." Because He lives, we may live also. Jesus said, "Whosoever liveth and believeth in Me shall never die" (John 11:26). He invites us to come to Him. He urges "whosoever will" to "take the water of life freely" (Rev. 22:17).

If you don't know Jesus, you can come to know Him today because, according to Proverbs 9:1-6, He has set the table. All is ready. Just come. But you must come, as described in verse 4, as one who is simple. Come as one who does not know what to do or how to do it. You must come as one who is weak, as one who is a sinner, as one who is undeserving. You must come not because you deserve to come, but because He has extended His arms of love and grace to you, an unworthy sinner. Jesus said, "Him that cometh to Me I will in no wise cast out" (John 6:37). If you come at His invitation, nobody is going to turn you away at the door. Come on in. Sit down freely. Salvation in Christ will admit you to immediate fellowship with Him. Sit down and enjoy the food at His table.

Unwise to Reprove a Scorner

Let's move on. Verses 7-9 of chapter 9 read, "He that reproveth a scorner getteth to himself shame, and he that rebuketh a wicked man getteth himself a blot. Reprove not a scorner [or a scoffer], lest he hate thee; rebuke a wise man, and he will love thee. Give instruction to a wise man, and he will be yet wiser; teach a just man, and he will increase in learning."

Many of us do not like criticism. Upon being criticized, we immediately become defensive and as a result we never learn to improve. I get a lot of unkind, critical mail every day. Twenty-five years ago, when I was young in the ministry, if I got a critical letter I fired back in like manner. But I have learned a bit about the Christian graces, and God has knocked off a few rough edges and given me some maturity in Christ.

If you are a sensitive Christian, you ought to feel an obligation in your heart to advise other Christian brothers and sisters when there is something in their lives that needs improving. Likewise, though it is more difficult, when someone suggests to you that same need, you are to take it in the spirit of love, knowing that this is God's way of making you a little more like Jesus. God desires to help us grow more and more into the image of Christ.

But Solomon reminds us not to reprove a scorner (v. 8). I have a friend, a former newsman named Cal Thomas. He is six feet, eight inches tall. As a vice-president of Moral Majority, he goes out and debates on university campuses across the country. In almost every audience there will be those people who are not going to be changed at all by facts. Their minds are made up. He frequently finds himself debating with a left-winger or some libertarian or someone who is in favor of abortion. He goes up against those who favor pornography on television, the antifamily forces, and homosexuals. He meets all kinds of people and experiences all kinds of audiences. As the debate goes on, some people in the audience will sit and "oink" like pigs. I mean they honestly "oink" aloud. Others will hiss like a snake. Sometimes they shout down my voice, and that of Cal Thomas, by yelling obscenities, vulgarities, and profanity—unprintable words.

Solomon said that we should not reprove that kind of person because he won't listen. When you try to help a person like that, he just becomes angry. I used to think I could reason with just about anybody. But in the last four years, I have talked with people who have no reasoning or logic because they are committed to a Christless, ungodly ideology. They do not want to hear anything else. So when you are dealing with scoffers and scorners who have a hidden agenda, you have to learn to live by the Word of God. We are to preach the Gospel and live for Jesus. Build a great Christian family. Get involved in a good Bible-believing church. Serve the Lord. Teach your children right from wrong. Teach them the traditional monogamous family. Teach them to treasure human life, unborn and born. Teach them the values of love. Teach them never to be prejudiced. Teach them to love everybody. That is the nobler, higher thing that God has called us to. But do not rebuke a scorner. You just waste your time.

The Beginning of Wisdom

Solomon teaches that "the fear of the Lord is the beginning of wisdom; and the knowledge of the holy is understanding. For by Me thy days shall be multiplied, and the years of thy life shall be increased. If thou be wise, thou shalt be wise for thyself, but if thou scornest, thou alone shalt bear it" (vv. 10-12). Yes, the best-educated person in any church, university, or business in all America—or the world, for that matter—is that person who truly knows the Word of God. That is because the ultimate education is to know the mind of God. The beginning of wisdom is the fear of the Lord, and the fear of the Lord is the beginning of wisdom.

Now if someone wants to be an atheist, that is his business, but God says in Psalm 14:1, "The fool hath said in his heart, There is no God." The atheist is a foolish person. Why? Because he does not even have the beginning of wisdom. If he does not believe there is a God, obviously he does not fear God. If he does not fear God, the Scripture says he is a fool, because fearing God is the beginning of wisdom.

Solomon goes on to say, "If thou be wise, thou shalt be wise for thyself" (Prov. 9:12). That means that wisdom is the reward in itself. You do not need to desire things when you really have Jesus as Lord of your life. God may give you things, but those things will never have a grip on you. When Jesus is Lord of your life, He is the most important person in your life. Right behind Him come your spouse and children and the rest of your family, and right behind them will be a lost world to whom you are committed. If, in the process, God puts clothes on your back, food in your mouth, and provides a house in which to live, that is just frosting on the cake. Those are fringe benefits. They are not necessary, but God is so kind He usually does those things too. And so we are told that God loves us, and wisdom is the reward in itself.

Beware, the Prostitute

In Proverbs 9:13-18 Solomon warns again against the prostitute. In that day, as in this one, sex was the god of some people. There are those people today who think that sex is purely animal instinct rather than the highest and noblest marriage act. We who are Christians believe, according to Hebrews 13, that sex is for the marriage bed only, and that it is to be within legal marriage only. But there are those today who literally scorn that statement. As mentioned earlier, they believe that bodies were made for exploitation, and that hedonism is the highest religion on earth. "If it feels good, do it." Well, according to Proverbs 9:13 and following, the foolish woman, the prostitute, is "simple." She knows nothing. She sits at the front door of her house (v. 14). She waits for men to go by. She beckons them in (v. 15). And verse 16 says that the dumb ones go in.

God intended marriage to be sacred. But it was not sacred to the simpleton in verses 16-17. "Stolen waters are sweet." That is the philosophy of the world. "Bread eaten in secret is pleasant." It may seem that way, but it is not true. There is no true, lasting satisfaction in illicit sex. It may seem exciting, but it leaves a hopeless trail of shame and guilt. "Whatsoever a man soweth, that shall he also reap" (Gal. 6:7).

Solomon's startling conclusion to the chapter is stated in Proverbs 9:18: "But he knoweth not that the dead are there." The man who goes in to a prostitute does not realize that others who have traveled the path before him are no longer around to tell about it. One translation says that what he does not realize is that all the former guests are now residents of hell. That is certainly a stiff price to pay for a fleeting moment of false pleasure. God so made men and women that monogamy—again, one man for one woman for one lifetime—is not only the ideal, but the only truly satisfying relationship.

Hold to Absolute Standards

Men, you need to hold to that absolute standard. Make sure you find all your satisfaction at home with your wife. Protect your mind. Get rid of the garbage, filthy magazines, and pictures that are so universal in America today. Exercise self-control over your conversation, the jokes you tell and listen to, and your television viewing habits. That will probably eliminate 90 percent of the prime-time television you might be watching.

Ladies, you need to make sure you adhere to God's standards of purity as well. There is plenty of filth available to the average housewife today too. You cannot walk out of the average supermarket without being bombarded with half tabloids with headlines that shout out a sexual message. Many of television's game shows and talk shows are punctuated with lewd suggestions and immoral overtones. The soap operas are simply cesspools of iniquity, and I do not mind saying that a Christian has no business watching them. In addition, the newspaper advice columns are laden with immoral situations and unbiblical suggestions. We need to raise up a generation of young people who will know God's standards and live by them. But that will be impossible unless adults first set the example.

5

Parental Advice from Solomon

Proverbs 10—12

A young university graduate who had studied child behavior used to lecture often on "The Ten Commandments for Parents." Later he married and became a father. He altered the title of his lecture to "Ten Hints for Parents." After a second child arrived, he spoke on "Some Suggestions for Parents." After a third child was born, he stopped lecturing altogether.

The advice that Solomon gives, however, needs no apology nor frequent revisions. Proverbs 10 lends itself to expository verse-by-verse teaching because it deals with so many different subjects. The home is spoken of first: "A wise son maketh a glad father, but a foolish son is the heaviness of his mother" (v. 1). Here Solomon is talking about the home and the relationship of parents and children. We have a 40 percent divorce rate in America today. One of the basic reasons for that, of course, is lack of teaching as to the sanctity and the preciousness of the home. Families are the backbone of any nation, and yet the American family unit is falling apart. The fiber and the fabric of America is disintegrating.

The Son Who Loves God

As a father I can testify that nothing makes me happier than a son who loves God, who is obedient and submissive to authority. Indeed, a wise son sees things from God's point of view and acts on things from God's perspective.

On the other hand, nothing breaks the heart of a mother like a foolish son (v. 1). The word *foolishness* or *foolish* in Proverbs either refers to a denial of the existence of God or rebellion against the Law of God. There is nothing that breaks a mother's heart like a rebellious son—a foolish son who rejects God and His teachings.

How we need to see to it that our children grow up in the nurture and admonition of the Lord in our homes! The size of the house is not the important thing. The amount of income is not the key factor. But the spiritual values that are taught are extremely important.

Verse 2 declares that "treasures of wickedness profit nothing." This is another way of saying "ill-gotten gain comes to naught." That is, money that is not earned by legal and moral means brings no true happiness and no lasting joy to the recipient. There are those who make careers of crime. They are dishonest and gain money by cheating other people. But God says the treasures of wickedness profit nothing. Here we have the Lord teaching us the value of the work ethic and the importance of honesty, integrity, and character building. May God help us in these days to come back to those principles and ethics.

One reason I oppose secular humanism so emphatically is that it destroys the Judeo-Christian ethic. Secular humanism presupposes there is no Creator God. It espouses evolution as its cardinal doctrine. According to this philosophy, man arrived here by accident. There is no God to whom he must one day give an account. When he dies, like an animal he ceases to exist. Therefore, between birth and death, since there is no Creator or Judge to whom man must report, situation ethics becomes his behavioral code. Eat, drink, and be merry, for tomorrow you die. Live as you please—you will give no account. Secular humanism, situation ethics, and the philosophy of no absolutes will ultimately destroy our society. We must stand against that tide.

This is one reason I am so strongly in favor of the return of voluntary prayer to public schools. We need to acknowledge the existence of Almighty God. Our children need to acknowledge that there is a Supreme Being, that man did not get here by chance, and that we are here to glorify God. The secular humanist feels that man is the only measure of himself. He has created his own utopia. But utopianism in a fallen society always brings disaster. "One nation under God" must be more than a slogan or phrase we repeat unconsciously in our pledge of allegiance to our flag. "Treasures of wickedness profit nothing, but righteousness [right living] delivereth from death" (v. 2). That applies to our nation as well.

The Righteous Will Not Starve
We move now from the family to the work ethic. Verse 3 declares, "The Lord will not suffer the soul of the righteous to famish." That is, God will not allow a right-living person to starve to death. That is a marvelous promise. We may lose a little weight. Most of us can afford that. We may suffer a little, but somehow—just as God delivered the Prophet Elijah—God will bring us the raven too. God will bring the food and provide the need, unless it is His will and time to take us home. But this third verse has a corollary: "The Lord will not suffer the soul of the righteous to famish, but He casteth away the substance of the wicked." That which is obtained by dishonest and unscriptural means will vanish.

"He becometh poor that dealeth with a slack hand, but the

hand of the diligent maketh rich" (v. 4). Poverty comes to those who are lazy. The fellow who wants to get something for nothing will become poor. The hard-working man who gets up early and goes down late and works five and six days a week will earn enough to provide for his family.

Frequently, I am in debates and hear people talking about socialism, communism, capitalism, and free enterprise as though all of them are just concepts and any one of them is as good as the other. That is ridiculous. The right of private property ownership is as biblical as John 3:16. Communism is nothing more than slavery, with the state owning everything and everybody. And socialism is the first cousin of communism. I wish everyone would read Harold Lindsell's book *Free Enterprise: A Judeo-Christian Defense* (Tyndale). It shows the scriptural basis for the free enterprise system in an excellent manner.

"Make Hay While the Sun Shines"
"He that gathereth in summer is a wise son" (v. 5). Or: A wise son will make hay while the sun shines. He will work while it is yet day, because the night comes when no man can work. He will work while he is physically able to do it. But by way of contrast, "he that sleepeth in harvest is a son that causes shame" (v. 5). The shameful son misses the opportunities when they come by. Really good opportunities do not often knock twice. God sometimes gives you an open door. He speaks to you about the opportunity, but because you slept too late or did not feel up to it at the moment or did not go against your flesh and your feelings, somebody else got the opportunity.

The so-called class struggles you hear about in the media today are designed to take from those who have and give to those who have not. Called "redistributing the wealth" by those who sponsor the concept, in reality this is nothing more than sharing poverty equally. This doctrine is wicked and poisonous. Scripture clearly teaches that we have the right to work hard, to achieve, to own, to earn, to accomplish, and that no one has the right to take our achievements away. When God does bless us with things, we ought to share with others. But the Communist idea of revolution, conspiracy, and murder being spawned today is designed to wipe out free enterprise and freedom itself. The key word is *freedom.*

Verse 6 says, "Blessings are upon the head of the just, but violence covereth the mouth of the wicked." Following God's plans as outlined in the Bible and moving in accordance with His will brings blessing.

"The memory of the just is blessed" (v. 7). I thank God for those just ones who have lived down through the ages—Noah, Abraham, Moses, David. I think of Luther, Moody, and Billy Sunday. Thank God for the just men of these past 6,000 years of human history. Crooks and thieves and the abominable are soon forgotten and lost in the dust. That is exactly what the Scripture says in the last half of verse 7, "The name of the wicked shall rot."

"The wise in heart will receive commandments" (v.8). A wise person will be instructed. All of life is learning. My friend Coach Tom Landry could tell you that in football over the last thirty-five years everything has changed. An athlete who is not open to learning and mastering new techniques is not going to make it. That is true with Christians as well. Any parent, Christian businessman, or leader must continually be learning and taking in new information to develop, grow, and mature. But a prating or babbling fool who refuses to listen to anybody else will fall (v. 8). I run into those prating fools everywhere. They are usually demonstrating up and down the streets, waving their banners, using profanity, and cursing. The Bible says they are doomed to failure.

By contrast, verse 9 says, "He that walketh uprightly [with stability] walketh surely." If you walk according to the Word of God, you will stand, but "he that perverteth his ways shall be known" (v. 9). "He that winketh with the eye [ignores sin] causeth sorrow, but a prating fool shall fall" (v. 10).

Solomon said that " the mouth of a righteous man is a well of life" (v. 11). That pictures an artesian spring. People will come to hear a man who lives for God and loves God. They will listen when he speaks, "but violence covereth the mouth of the wicked" (v. 11).

Verse 12 warns that hatred stirs up strifes, but points out that love covers all sins. This world needs a baptism of love. There is so much hatred today. When President Reagan was shot, news flashed across the land and around the world. When the announcement was made over the PA system in a certain school, applause and cheering followed. That is an indictment against the parents of those children. They were merely reflecting their parents' attitude. May God deliver us from hatred and help us love people—even those who hate us!

"In the lips of him that hath understanding wisdom is found, but a rod is for the back of him that is void of understanding. Wise men lay up knowledge" (vv. 13-14). Wise men learn and accumulate knowledge. Wise men memorize truths, "but the mouth of the foolish is near destruction. The rich man's wealth is his strong city" (vv. 14-15). He leans on it. Too many times the man who has been blessed materially lets wealth become his god. On the other hand, "the destruction of the poor is their poverty" (v. 15). Others allow poverty to become their bitterness and that also destroys them. There is nothing wrong with possessing things. But there is something very wrong with things possessing you. There is nothing wrong with God trusting things into your hands, if you are using them for the glory of God.

Notice Proverbs 10:16: "The labor [income] of the righteous tendeth to life." The income is invested into the cause of Christ. The righteous man is blessed materially, and therefore his labor, his earnings, are tending to life. They are invested in carrying forth the Gopel.

We have dealt with the family, the work ethic, stewardship, and interpersonal relationships. Now notice verse 22: "The blessing of the Lord, it maketh rich, and He addeth no sorrow with it." If you want to prosper and be successful in your work—whether it is business, ministry, athletics, or particularly in your home—you need the blessing of the Lord. To have the blessing of the Lord, you must follow the principles of God's Word, and as we go through Proverbs in this study, we are discovering those principles. I wish we could cover every verse, but that just is not possible in these pages.

Notice verse 30: "The righteous shall never be removed, but the wicked shall not inhabit the earth." We hear a lot about social security these days. I believe in the Social Security system. I think we should take care of the aged and the indigent and those who cannot help themselves. But did you know that the only true social security in the world is to be in the will of God? But may I say to you, Uncle Sam is not your security. Only the Lord is. Only God can go with you everywhere, take care of you, provide your needs, and protect you. And if you know Jesus as your personal Saviour, He lives in your heart and the Spirit of God indwells you. Furthermore, God's angels are encamped round about you (Ps. 34:7), and you can claim the promise, "My God shall supply all your need according to His riches in glory by Christ Jesus" (Phil. 4:19).

Spiritual Attributes

There are several key verses in Proverbs 11. First, consider verse 14: "Where no counsel is, the people fall, but in the multitude of counselors, there is safety." Another key verse is "As righteousness tendeth to life, so he that pursueth evil pursueth it to his own death" (v. 19). Then verses 24-25 tie together as a key thought. "There is that scattereth, and yet increaseth; and there is that withholdeth more than is meet, but it tendeth to poverty. The liberal soul shall be made fat, and he that watereth shall be watered also himself." The final key verse is verse 30: "The fruit of the righteous is a tree of life, and he that winneth souls is wise."

The entire chapter may be divided into seven sections.

● In verses 1-8 Solomon treats honesty. Verse 1 says, "A false balance is abomination to the Lord, but a just weight is His delight." That is another way of saying that God hates cheating, lying, and dishonesty. God loves integrity and honesty. "A just weight is His delight." It is important to be honest in our relationships with ourselves, our families, other people, and with God. We only fool ourselves when we live dishonestly. For example, verse 2 says be honest about who we are: "When pride cometh, then cometh shame." We should not think too highly of ourselves. In verse 3 we are told, "The integrity of the upright shall guide them." If you follow principles of integrity in every undertaking, they will guide you in making the kinds of decisions that will bring the blessings of God upon you. Verse 4 tells us why: "Riches profit not in the day of wrath." That means money will not do you any good on the Day of Judgment. When you stand before God, you will stand before Him just like everybody else—poor, empty, naked, just as you were when you came into the world.

● Verses 9-13 talk about influence. "An hypocrite with his mouth destroyeth his neighbor". A gossiper, a slanderer, hurts people. "But through knowledge shall the just be delivered. When it goeth well with the righteous, the city rejoiceth; and when the wicked perish, there is shouting" (vv. 9-10).

But verse 11 is the key verse: "By the blessing of the upright the city is exalted." Jesus said, "Ye are the salt of the earth" (Matt. 5:13). Salt gives flavor and preserves. The saints of God sprinkled in a community will bring blessing upon the entire community. One reason why America has been so blessed of God is that there are more saints of God per capita in America than you will find anywhere else in the world. And these grains of salt have prevented America from spoiling morally. The majority of people in this country are for what is right, and the saints of God are blessing the community. "By the blessing of the upright the city [or the nation] is exalted" (Prov. 11:11).

● Verse 14 declares: "Where no counsel is, the people fall, but in the multitude of counselors there is safety." That means that without wise leadership a nation is in serious trouble. I thank God for a President who is trying to get prayer back in schools, trying to stop abortion, and working hard to get nonpublic education advanced in this nation through tuition tax credits which prevent double taxation of parents because they send their children to private schools. I just pray that someday God will give us a Congress, a Supreme Court, 50 governors, and state legislators who will stand up for what is right on every issue and for what the Word of God teaches. Leadership is the key. I am thankful also for the preachers who are taking their stand for what is right these days.

● Now consider verses 15-21 and the subject of kindness. "He that is surety for a stranger shall smart for it; and he that hateth suretyship is sure" (v. 15). As mentioned in chapter 3 of this book, this simply means that it is not wise to sign a note for a person who may not be able to pay his loans. You are kinder in the long run to avoid unsecured loans—kinder to your friend, your family, yourself.

"The merciful man doeth good to his own soul, but he that

is cruel troubleth his own flesh" (v. 17). We need to learn kindness in our relationships with each other. A merciful man obtains mercy. If we expect to have the friendship of the people around us, we must show ourselves friendly. This is a day when employers, employees, parents, businessmen and women, politicians, and leaders need to learn to respect one another as peers. We need to show kindness in every situation, because verse 20 says, "They that are of a froward [rebellious] heart are abomination to the Lord." And, "Though hand join in hand [as in a conspiracy], the wicked shall not be unpunished" (vv. 20-21).

● Verses 22 and 23 emphasize the importance of living by God's moral principles. "As a jewel of gold in a swine's snout, so is a fair woman which is without discretion" (v. 22). That is another way of saying that a big twenty-carat diamond in a pig's snout is just as out of place as a beautiful woman who does not live a clean, moral, discreet, and chaste life. Hollywood is an example of the pig's snout. Many cheap Hollywood magazines carry ongoing stories of love affairs between those who have already had three or four husbands or wives and are now lusting after another one. The behavior is a lot like animals. That is the standard of Hollywood. Morality is still the right way—God's way.

● Verses 24-28 express the principle of stewardship. "There is that scattereth, and yet increaseth" (v. 24). As we learn to give to others and take what God gives to us and scatter it to those in need, what we have left will increase. I have proved that principle by experience. I learned to tithe the week after I was saved. I do not know how to explain it, but once I began tithing, what I had leftover went further than the entire amount used to go before I started tithing. I found that the more I scattered the more I increased. I dare you to try it. It works—it is biblical.

● Finally, notice verse 30 that speaks of reproduction: "The fruit of the righteous is a tree of life, and he that winneth souls is wise." This is reproduction. The most exciting thing I am involved in is training the young people at Liberty Baptist Schools and then watching them go out and start churches, assume churches, or build churches. They are leading thousands of souls to Christ and beginning to send their students to Liberty for training. May we have many like that. That is godly, biblical reproduction.

The Way to Conquer Discouragement

The Book of Proverbs gives God's recipe for a successful life, as pointed out earlier. God wants us to know the facts by which we can live happy, fulfilled, successful lives. Part of our success will come from meeting and conquering discouragement and depression. The key text in Proverbs 12 is verse 25: "Heaviness [discouragement] in the heart of man maketh it stoop." Dwight L. Moody, the great evangelist of the last century, said, "I have never known God to use a discouraged person." I agree. When you are discouraged, you are of no value to your family, to God, to your employer, or even to yourself. When you are discouraged, depressed, and defeated in your spirit, you are worthless. Now the problem with discouragement is that we never properly name it. It is not "emotional weakness" or merely a "vice." It is *sin*. Paul tells us that "whatsoever is not of faith is sin" (Rom. 14:23). Faith is the opposite of discouragement. Faith is taking God at His word no matter what the circumstances and believing what He has said.

Now there is a cure for sin: "The blood of Jesus Christ, His Son, cleanseth from all sin" (1 John 1:7). If we will come to God and call discouragement *sin*, and admit to it, we can have God's forgiveness. Then by faith, as we apply the principles of Proverbs 12, we can learn how to have victory in Christ to come up out of the valley and live that victorious life. Victory over sin can make you useful to God, to your family, to your employer, and to yourself. God wants you to be successful.

Now let us discover the principles in chapter 12 that can bring you out of discouragement and defeat. The chapter begins, "Whoso loveth instruction loveth knowledge, but he that hateth reproof is brutish [stupid]." I do not like to use the word *stupid* unless I really mean it. But this is exactly what Solomon says. If you are going to have victory over the problems and pressures of life and be a victorious Christian, you must be a learner. You need to be taking in the Word of God constantly by reading the Scriptures and hiding the Word of God in your heart. You must learn how to be rebuked by the Word as it is applied by the Holy Spirit or by other men and women in Christ.

A Christian is not to be a reservoir. The Dead Sea in Israel, the lowest point on the earth, has no life in it because, though it has an inlet, the Jordan River, it has no outlet. Christians who take in but don't give out will always be discouraged and defeated.

There is another principle in verses 2-3: "A good man obtaineth favor of the Lord, but a man of wicked devices will He condemn. A man shall not be established by wickedness, but the root of the righteous shall not be moved." You need to have certain anchors and roots in your life. We talk about the Judeo-Christian ethic. That is just another way of saying the principles of the Old and New Testaments. That ethic is an anchor. We say that this is "a nation under God," founded upon that ethic. I believe that. Most of our Presidents have believed that. Most of our members of Congress have believed that down through the years. But we have secular humanists in our society today who are trying to take us from "under God" and make this a secular nation.

Our nation needs to recall its heritage and a person needs

to have certain roots. He needs to know what he believes. Learn the principles of common decency and of the monogamous Christian home. Learn the dignity of human life, the principle of the work ethic, the Abrahamic covenant, God-centered education, and the divinely ordained institutions of home, state, and church. Learn these principles in your life and allow them to guide you. If you want to have victory over discouragement, you have to go with God. You cannot go against God.

A well-known man wrote me the other day, furious because of my support of the President toward putting prayer back in schools. He was also furious because of my oppostion to abortion and because I believe in biblical Creation. I told him that his problem is not with Jerry Falwell, because a majority of Americans agree with what I believe. I told him that his problem is with God Almighty.

Verse 4 says, "A virtuous woman is a crown to her husband." That speaks of morality. We are in a society today committed largely to immorality, as discussed earlier. The woman at the well at Sychar had been married five times and was living then with a man to whom she was not married (John 4:18). God forgave her and used her to bring a whole city to Christ. So do not despair if you have messed up your life in the past. Get God's forgiveness and go and sin no more, living by the principles of the Word of God.

Proverbs 12:6 speaks of violence: "The words of the wicked are to lie in wait for blood." If you are going to succeed in life, violence cannot be a part of it. Some people today violate the principles of common decency and of love and respect for their fellowman. Several years ago, Lebanon was overrun by PLO terrorists. When Israel went in and cleared out the PLO murderers and terrorists, they were criticized for it. But we need to stand by our friends. We need to stand against violence. That is exactly what Israel's action was all about stopping terrorists who were destroying men, women, and children. This world today is filled with violent people.

Then we have the "peaceniks" and the "freezeniks" too. I wish there had never been a nuclear bomb, but until there can be absolute, impeccable inspection and verification of what the Soviets are doing, I support the President in peace through strength. May God help us guarantee that our children grow up in a free society. We all hate war, but the only way to guarantee that the Soviets do not encamp on our soil, as they have in Poland and Afghanistan and elsewhere, is to be so strong they do not dare to come.

There is another principle in verse 16: "A fool's wrath is presently known." A fool has a quick temper. A fool's wrath is presently or quickly known. If you are going to have victory over discouragement, you have to have victory over your emotions. As soon as a boxer gets angry, the next thing he sees are the lights glaring down on him. His wrath gets him in trouble. As I have mentioned, I frequently take part in debates. Anybody who debates knows that the moment you get angry, you lose. What you really want to do to win a debate is to get the other fellow angry. When he is spitting and sputtering and frothing at the mouth, just smile at him.

One time on "Donahue" I was debating two ACLU lawyers and a vice-president of the American Federation of Teachers. They always make it about three to one. I guess they figure it takes three of them to equal one of us! But they got angry and went into orbit. The crowd immediately came over to my side. Even an atheist woman called in to say she was for silent prayer! If you want to be happy and victorious in life, do not be a victim of your emotions. Do not say things you need to repent of later. Look to the Lord. When you are really uptight, the best thing to do is head into the next room, otherwise you will probably say something you will have to go back and apologize for later. So get control of your emotions.

And finally, verse 24 says, "The hand of the diligent shall bear rule, but the slothful shall be under tribute." If you are going to have victory over discouragement, work hard. The greatest cure for discouragement and depression is productivity. Do something worthwhile: help somebody; build something; go out and find your place of ministry. I always advise our senior saints never to retire. You may quit doing a certain job, but do not ever retire.

A preacher of the Gospel could never retire. He might have to preach from a nursing home, but he will witness, preach, and share as long as there is breath left in him. You may have to stop working at a particular job by legal requirement, but do something. Keep doing and keep going; never stop. Work hard, and do not ever let anybody tell you that hard work is going to kill you. You may die working to get out of work. Most of the people I know do not *work* themselves to death. They *worry* themselves to death.

Get in there and work according to the abilities God gives, and that old heart will not be heavy. The best way I know to keep from discouragement is to share Christ with others. All discouragement flees when I have the job of opening the Scriptures to Romans 10:9-10, 13 so that someone may call upon the name of the Lord and get saved through believing in the death, burial, and resurrection of Christ. No matter how I felt before that soul-winning experience, I leave there on cloud nine because one more person is ready for the kingdom of heaven. When we live by God's principles, we will not be discouraged, defeated, and depressed.

6

Living Right in God's Service
Proverbs 13—15

For years I have loved and read Andrew Murray, the great South African preacher who died in 1917. He had eleven children grow to adulthood. Five sons became ministers, and four of his daughters became ministers' wives. In the following generation, ten of his grandsons became preachers and another thirteen were missionaries. The secret of his unusual contribution to the Christian ministry was to be found in his home life. Consistent godly living in the home brought certain results.

Solomon's advice if rightly followed will also yield pleasant fruit. Proverbs 13 contains 25 verses, and each verse presents a key to help us in our daily living. The chapter begins, "A wise son heareth his father's instruction, but a scorner heareth not rebuke." Beside that verse in my Bible I have written, "Parental authority."

Right Relationships

● *Chain of command*—I do not know of a biblically successful man anywhere in the world who does not recognize the principle of the biblical chain of command as it relates to the family and the home. The real need in America today is to rebuild and to build great families in which the mother and father are rightly related to God and each other.

In my almost thirty years as a pastor, I have conducted hundreds of weddings, maybe thousands. Now it is not unusual for me to marry the children of those I had the privilege of marrying earlier in my ministry. To see young people grow up and get married and still love and respect their parents is wonderful. And to see those parents still in the place God wants them to be is a great blessing.

● *Reason and Logic*—The second principle points to the need for reason and logic. "A man shall eat good by the fruit of his mouth, but the soul of the transgressors shall eat violence" (v. 2). The good man, the man of God, wins not by physical violence but by careful argument. He understands and can properly present the facts.

On the debate circuit, we are usually to the right—politically and morally speaking—of the one we debate. The audience is usually stacked against us too. But we have scriptural principles that have not changed. We have a God whose character has never changed. We have a message and a ministry that we do not have to change with the times. Our hostile friends in the audience may scream and shout all kinds of obscenities and vulgar expressions, and there may be unfair practices on the platform. But we have learned that by the civil presentation of facts, people who listen with open minds understand. We do not ever have to revert to violence, verbal or physical. We can always go by the principles of verse 2—reason and logic.

● *Self-control*—Solomon's third key to daily living is self-control. Verse 3 says, "He that keepeth his mouth keepeth his life." Self-control means controlling the tongue. That little tongue, James tells us, is one of the smallest parts of our body, and yet, like the rudder on a ship, it turns a mighty amount of weight (James 3:4). If all of us were as good at listening as we are at talking, we would be very intelligent. But most of us are not. We need to allow the indwelling Holy Spirit, who gives the nine virtues of the Spirit (Gal. 5:22-23), to give self-control to monitor our tongues. The fruit of the Spirit is love, joy, peace, long-suffering, gentleness, goodness, faith, meek-ness, and the last one is temperance, or self-control.

● *Diligence*—Our fourth principle for living relates to work: "The soul of the sluggard [lazy person] desireth, and hath nothing, but the soul of the diligent shall be made fat" (Prov. 13:4). Here, Solomon stresses *diligence*. One of the principles of the Judeo-Christian ethic is the work ethic. The idea that man is owed a living because he belongs to the human race is not biblical. The very first chapters of Genesis make it clear that by the sweat of our brow we earn our bread (Gen. 3:18-19). Paul told us that if a man will not work, neither shall he eat (2 Thes. 3:10). That does not mean that we have no compassion and concern for the indigent, the sick, the helpless, the aged, and those who cannot work. But it does teach us the value and the preciousness of the work ethic and that we are supposed to work if we are able and if we want to eat.

In Virginia, where I live, there are many summer agricul-tural jobs. The minimum wage or a bit higher is paid. When the Virginia Employment Commission contacted the unem-ployed about these jobs, there was little response except that the jobs were too hard and the pay too low. These jobs are obviously not too hard and the pay too low for those foreign and migrant workers who flock into the state to grab the jobs that Virginians will not have. Just as obviously, there are many unemployed people in this state who do not want to work if that means working up a sweat. They would rather draw unemployment compensation for which they have not con-

tributed a cent and/or welfare benefits for which some
else who *is* working has to pay. We need to take our stand
the work ethic and teach our boys and girls to be diligent

• *Honesty and fairness*—Now, notice another principl
for living in verse 5: "A righteous man hateth lying, but a
wicked man is loathsome, and cometh to shame." That is
another way of saying a good man hates dishonesty, and
wicked men live in dishonesty. We need to operate by the
principles of honesty and fairness. The Golden Rule is still,
"Do unto others as you would have them do unto you" (see
Matt. 7:12). It is not—as I read in one of the major newspa-
pers the other day—"He who has the gold makes the rules."
That is not the biblical perspective.

I am frequently contacted by the press to comment on
what someone else said. But in all fairness to the individual, I
cannnot comment without asking him what he actually said.
We are often misquoted and have our comments taken
completely out of context. I sometimes read about what I
supposedly said somewhere, and it does not resemble in the
least what I said. Yet, some of the "brethren" are quick to take
comments they read in the secular or even the religious press
without any question as to their validity. All one has to do to
be honest and fair is to contact the individual to determine if
what was reported is true or not. Our national news media is
often biased and unfair because of its liberal mindset. Christians do not need to believe everything they hear or read
until they are sure of the facts. Let us be fair and honest with
others.

• *"Principled living"*—The sixth key to daily living is
"principled living." Verse 6 says, "Righteousness keepeth him
that is upright in the way." We need to know the principles of
the Word of God and live by those principles. This requires
Bible study and a devotional life of prayer.

• *True values*—"There is that maketh himself rich, yet hath

maketh himself poor, yet hath great
we have the principle of developing true
teaches that you can be very poor and still
have the right value system, money does not
very high. I could take you around the world and
to you.

wardship—Verse 8 declares, "The ransom of a man's
his riches, but the poor heareth not rebuke." The key
is stewardship. A poor man does not have to worry
about being kidnapped, because nobody wants to kidnap a
poor person for ransom. That is all verse 8 means. It really
suggests that the best things in life are free. There are plenty
of blessings in every station in life if we care to look for them.

● *Walk in God's light*—Verse 9 says, "The lamp of the
wicked shall be put out." We are to walk in the light of the
Word of God. As we do, it will be a constant light to our path
(Ps. 119:105), and as the psalmist says, "The entrance of Thy
words giveth light" (Ps. 119:130).

● *Humililty*—The key in verse 10 is humility: "Only by
pride cometh contention, but with the well advised is wisdom." There is no such thing as a great man who does not
know humility. The greatest people I know could not be
picked out in a crowd. They are just regular people. There
are no big shots in the fraternity of the great.

● *Sacrificial living*—"Wealth gotten by vanity [gambling]
shall be diminished, but he that gathereth by labor shall
increase (v. 11). The old-timers had it right: "Easy come, easy
go." If we learn to work hard for what we get, we appreciate
it and handle it more meticulously.

● *Hope*—Verse 12 talks of the key of hope. "Hope deferred
maketh the heart sick." How wonderful it is to have hope.
The Word of God and our walk with Christ gives us that silver lining on every rainbow. We have the promise of heaven
when this life is over. That is the hope above all others.

● *Obedience*—Another important key is obedience to the Word of God. "Whoso despiseth the Word shall be destroyed" (v. 13). Obey the Word of God, or be destroyed.

● *Listen to counsel*—The word *counsel* is the key to verse 14: "The law of the wise is a fountain of life." We need to listen to godly men and women to learn to live more successfully, especially to those who are older and have been through life.

● *Common sense*—Verse 15 says, "Good understanding giveth favor, but the way of transgressors is hard." Here the key words are *common sense.* Common sense is the best education available to anybody. There are many with several degrees who lack common, practical, horse sense. May God help us as we read the Word and as we live with people to learn common sense.

● *Planning*—Verse 16 expresses the key thought of planning: "Every prudent man dealeth with knowledge, but a fool layeth open his folly." Learn to plan; prudent men plan. There is nothing unspiritual about planning. Often, we plan for an event or a program a year or even two years in advance. When we short our planning, we usually end up hurting ourselves and others around us.

● *Communication*—"A wicked messenger falleth into mischief, but a faithful ambassador is health" (v. 17). Here the key word is *communication.* Learn to communicate with people. Listen to what they are saying, and learn how to say to others what you want to have said to you. Do not try to shut off debate. Do not try to censor people.

● *Constructive criticism*—Verse 18 reads, "Poverty and shame shall be to him that refuseth instruction, but he that regardeth reproof shall be honored." This teaches us about constructive criticism. We need to learn to to take criticism properly and to learn from it. We are often too good at giving it out but cannot receive it. Solomon says that when we give heed to reproof, we shall be honored.

● *Goals*—Setting and reaching goals is the theme of verse 19: "The desire accomplished is sweet to the soul." How good it is to have achieved a goal, to feel the pressure lift, and then to be able to move on to new heights.

● *Association*—The importance of your associations is emphasized in verse 20: "He that walketh with wise men shall be wise, but a companion of fools shall be destroyed." Do you want to be wise? Then associate with wise men. A good leader will never be afraid of top-notch talent but will seek to surround himself with the very best people he can find. But the opposite is true also: bad companions will tear one down and bring eventual destruction.

● *Reaping*—Verse 21 teaches that you will reap whatever you sow. "Evil pursueth sinners, but to the righteous good shall be repaid." This is an eternal Law of God and is often repeated in the Bible. Numbers 32:23 says, "Be sure your sin will find you out," and Galatians 6:7 says that whatsoever you sow, that shall you also reap. There is no way to get around it. To make sure your harvest is good, take care what you sow.

● *A godly legacy*—The key thought of verse 22—"A good man leaveth an inheritance to his children's children."—is the legacy we leave to our children and grandchildren. When the text speaks of an inheritance, we usually think of money. But we leave behind more than that. Let us strive to leave a godly heritage to those who follow in our families.

● *Injustice*—Verse 23 speaks of social injustice and of reacting against it. We need to stand up for those who cannot help themselves and are being oppressed by others.

● *Discipline*—Effective discipline is the key in verse 24: "He that spareth the rod hateth his son, but he that loveth him chasteneth him betimes [early]." Real love will result in effective discipline, in spite of Dr. Spock. Children must be corrected by their parents before they begin to correct their parents. Children will know whether we correct them and apply the rod out of love, or whether we do it in anger. Make sure love rules your disciplining.

● *Right motivations*—Finally, we come to verse 25: "The righteous eateth to the satisfying of his soul, but the belly of the wicked shall want." That is a way of saying the good man eats to live, while the evil man lives to eat. Be motivated by the right things.

A Call to Christian Service

The Book of Proverbs, as pointed out, is designed to teach all of us how to live successfully according to the will and the Word of God. The ultimate of Christian wisdom is coming to that point in life where you can see things from God's vantage point. In Proverbs 14, we have a call to Christian service. The chapter has four divisions.

● The first division (vv. 1-4) deals with the high price of dedicated Christian service. It costs something to serve God. God never promised a life of ease and luxury. God never promised benefits and privileges. He simply said to take up your cross and follow Him. He has promised His presence, His provision, and His peace, but He has never promised a road of ease.

Verse 4 is an interesting verse to think about: "Where no oxen are, the crib is clean, but much increase is by the strength of the ox." If the farmer had no cattle, he could keep his barn clean, but if he did not have any cattle he would not even need a barn. Now, children can at times be tremendous problems to parents, but if there were no children, there would be no parents. There would be no need for parents. We have three children in our home. Macel and I have said many times, "Oh, this house is a mess. This place is wrecked! There is never a moment's peace here. These children are driving us nuts!" But, oh, thank God they do. It would be terrible to grow up in a house with no children around to tear up things and break furniture and wake you when you are trying to rest and disturb you when you are trying to think.

In the same way, evangelism, a phase of Christian service, is a serious problem for churches. If we could get out of the evangelism business, we would not have little, dirty-faced, barefooted children running around sticking gum under the seats and tearing up our hymnbooks and making noises while we try to teach, preach, and worship. But thank God for the little children!

Taking a stand for Christ will cost you something outside the church too. At your workplace, you may be considered a holy Joe, a fanatic. You do not flip for the drink, or read the dirty magazines and books. You do not drink booze with the crowd. You do not attend the parties where they carouse with other men's wives, and so on. Suddenly, you find out that taking a stand sometimes is a little bit lonely, and sometimes there is criticism. If you want everybody for you, just know nothing, do nothing, and have nothing. Then nobody will bother you.

● Now, notice the importance of Christian service in verses 5-12. Verse 9 says, "Fools make a mock at sin." We must take our stand for the Lord in these days because amoralists and secular humanists are trying to destroy the very existence of a Judeo-Christian ethic. Another reason it is important to serve God is that "the house of the wicked shall be overthrown" (v. 11). And, "There is a way which seemeth right unto a man, but the end thereof are the ways of death" (v. 12). I believe that there is a burning, literal hell where lost persons will spend a conscious, suffering eternity. And because I believe that, I must preach the death, the burial, and the resurrection of Christ in season and out of season

● The third point concerns the quality of Christian service

(vv. 13-25). The call to Christian service must have quality. The last half of verse 15 says that "the prudent man looketh well to his going." We must be holy people. Preaching and declaring the message is not enough. We must live the message. We must walk with God. We must practice what we preach. And in our daily lives the world must see Jesus in us.

Verse 18 says that "the prudent are crowned with knowledge." We should hide the Word of God away in our hearts.

Verses 20 and 21 tell us, "The poor is hated even of his own neighbor, but the rich hath many friends. He that despiseth his neighbor sinneth, but he that hath mercy on the poor, happy is he." We must be compassionate. We must have extended arms and hearts of love to those who are less fortunate than we. The quality of our commitment will be demonstrated by our treatment of the poor, the forsaken, and the disenfranchised.

Verse 25 says, "A true witness delivereth souls." We are to be soul-winners. J.O. Grooms is soul-winning director at Thomas Road Baptist Church. God uses him to lead thousands to Christ every year; but every one of us are to be soul-winners.

● Finally, look at the results of Christian service in verses 26-35. "In the fear of the Lord is strong confidence" (v. 26). God can give you that inner peace you need. He can give you the strength and grace you need to live successfully and happily. You do not have to endure life. You can enjoy life. In fact, "the fear of the Lord is a fountain of life" (v. 27). Not only can we enjoy life through victory in Christ now, we can have a home in heaven later. Who has a better retirement plan than that? Where are there better fringe benefits than heaven with the Lord forever and God's protection and presence right now?

And verse 34, "Righteousness exalteth a nation, but sin is a reproach to any people." We have the privilege of turning a nation around. I believe that the hope of America lies in the pulpits and pews of this country. If the people of God in this nation will take their stand for right and be willing to pay the price and answer the call to Christian service, I believe we can turn America around. And from that beginning, I believe we can give the Gospel to the 4.7 billion souls in this world in our generation. Let us get involved in Christian service!

"Talking Right and Living Right"

A good title for Proverbs 15 is "Talking Right and Living Right." There are three key verses in the chapter.

● The first key verse is 13: "A merry heart maketh a cheerful countenance, but by sorrow of the heart the spirit is broken." This says that a happy heart is reflected in a happy face. In any crowd we can discover where the happy heart is because there will also be a happy face looking at us. Now that does not mean that everything is always going the way you would like for it to go. But when the blessed Holy Spirit of God indwells a person, and when Jesus is Lord of that life, there is a spiritual contentment and peace that radiates right through the countenance. Any preacher who constantly looks at faces and preaches to audiences has learned how to pick out those people who really have found not only peace with God, but the peace of God that passes all understanding. Some look to the bottle for peace and happiness. Some search for it in pills, barbiturates, and heroin. Others look for it in hedonism, the worship of pleasure. But the only place they will find true happiness is in the living Christ, who indwells every born-again believer.

● The second key verse is 17: "Better is a dinner of herbs where love is, than a stalled [fattened] ox and hatred therewith." This is another way of saying that it is better to be eating vegetable soup with somebody who loves you than T-bone steak with somebody who hates you. Unfortunately, the latter is often what has happened to the family in America today. How beautiful or how large the home is, or how plush its furnishings are does not really matter. How much money there is in the bank is of little concern. If the love of God is not in the hearts of that family, and if love is not reflected by respect and the kinds of little things that really constitute a loving and stable home, then all the money in the world does not bring joy and happiness into that environment.

I read recently that a prominent person known to the television world put a gun to his head and killed himself. It was not because he was out of money, but because he was out of joy. Every day you read of the Hollywood stars who decide they have lived long enough with this wife or that husband. Next comes the divorce, and then the third wife, the fourth wife, and the tenth wife. It seems as if all the major magazines and newscasters honor and glamorize those persons who have been the most dishonorable in their family lives.

● The third key verse is the last verse of the chapter: "The fear of the Lord is the instruction of wisdom, and before honor is humility" (v. 33). If you are going to be great with God and great with men, you must learn humility—how to wash feet. Humble yourself—do the dirty jobs. Let the other fellow go first. Do most of the listening and very little of the talking. Know very little, and let everybody else know everything. Those are the kinds of great people that Solomon says the world needs.

Talking Right

Now let's consider the theme of talking right.

● "A soft answer turneth away wrath, but grievous words stir up anger" (Prov. 15:1). Why is it that some people get along in their interpersonal relationships with almost everybody, while others get along with virtually nobody? With some people, no matter where they are or what kind of work they do, if they are there long enough, there will be turmoil. Others, however, experience a perfect meshing and correlating of personalities, and the result is warmth and acceptance. What is the difference? I think the difference is in Matthew 5:9, "Blessed are the peacemakers." You do not need to prove that you were right and he was wrong. When others are unfair to you or when somebody usurps your authority, you do not have to respond with a blast. I have admired President Reagan's calmness under the constant attack of the liberal press and media. When you are attacked, you do not need to answer in kind.

● Verse 2 of Proverbs 15 says that "the tongue of the wise useth knowledge aright." Learn how to be skillful in the use of knowledge. Learn what the facts are and then how to disseminate them to others. It is amazing how many Christians do not know what they believe and why they believe it. Learn biblical doctrine, including the deity of Christ and the doctrine of salvation. Learn about the inspiration of Scripture. Learn the Word of God and study how to give those facts to others. I recommend that Christians read at least one good news magazine every week. Read at least one good daily newspaper every day. Find out what is happening in the world. You may find out that we are in a battle against secular humanists, and the battle is raging. Find out about the national sin of America—abortion. Find out about the pornographic explosion. Find out about the homosexual revolution. Find out what's happening in our country, and learn what you can do by using the Word of God properly. If you have not read Francis Schaeffer's *A Christian Manifesto* (Crossway), get a copy, read it, and find out the facts.

● "A wholesome tongue is a tree of life" (v. 4). Engage in healthy conversation that encourages and lifts up people. Learn how to be positive. Learn how to talk right. "A word spoken in due season, how good is it!" (v. 23) There are some people who will cross your path today, tonight, tomorrow, who just need a word from you to learn how to live and get over the hump. Right now someone is just about to throw in the towel. The right word from you at the right time can make the difference. Learn how to compliment people, and tell them when they are doing something right. Learn how to help people up, not down.

How to Live

Besides speaking about our conversation, Solomon talks about how to live. Verse 8 says that "the sacrifice of the wicked is an abomination to the Lord." You cannot work your way to heaven. Salvation is of the Lord. Solomon would teach us several things.

● First of all, the sacrifice of the wicked, the unsaved man, cannot please God. You can join every church, give all your money to the poor, but that will not save you. I read of wealthy people who die and leave a lot of money to this school or that foundation. Perhaps they think their gifts may get them into heaven. That will not get anybody in.

Let me add in passing that if you are a Christian, you ought to know where your money is going after you leave for heaven. You should not give a dime to a school that has professors in it who are teaching young people that the Bible is not the Word of God. You ought to find out where your money is going. The people of God in this country could build Christian schools that could change the society of our day if their money went into the right channels. But unfortunately, good people often support bad causes.

● Verse 9 says, "The way of the wicked is an abomination unto the Lord." Not only can you do nothing to obtain salvation except believe on Jesus and what He has done, but you cannot live the Christian life in the flesh. No man in the flesh can please God. You cannot do anything to honor God after you have become a Christian unless you do it in the power of the indwelling Holy Spirit. You cannot live the Christian life by your own works any more than you could work your way to heaven.

● Verse 26 goes on to say: "The thoughts of the wicked are an abomination to the Lord." The philosophy of the unregenerate can never honor God. What is secular humanism? It is the opposite of the Christian dynamic. What is the Christian dynamic? It is that Christ is central, and that man was created for God's pleasure, lives for God's pleasure, and one day will stand before God to give an account for how he has lived on this earth. Jesus Christ is the Centerpiece of the Christian dynamic. What is humanism? It is that man is an end in himself. He is his own utopia and the ultimate measure of all things. That is why the philosophy of the wicked is an abomination to the Lord. We need to begin thinking God's way. That is why we need to read the right Book, the Word of God. We need to be in God's house at all the services. We need to spend a lot of time in prayer. We need to spend time in the fellowship of the saints of God. On the other hand, we need to stay away from the garbage pits. We need to stay away from those places and things that would cause us to think the philosophy of the world. That is why our sons and daughters ought to go to distinctively Christian schools where everybody believes the Genesis account of Creation, the inspiration of the Word of God, salvation by grace, and all the principles and doctrines of the Word of God.

In conclusion, living and talking right involve the totality of our beings and our existence. They are not some insignificant matters on the periphery of our lives. We must give ourselves wholly to the task if we would talk right and live right for our Saviour. He died for us. Let us live for Him.

7

How to Build Proper Relationships
Proverbs 16—18

Psychologists tell us that about 10,000 thoughts pass through the human brain each day. That makes 70,000 each week, and 3.65 million thoughts a year. Jesus said that we would have to give an account of every idle word in the Day of Judgment (Matt. 12:36). Since that is the case, we had better learn how to control our thoughts and the words that result from those thoughts.

Controlling Your Thought Life
Proverbs 16 has a lot to say about controlling our thoughts. There is a battle going on today to capture the minds of our generation. As Christians, we must learn the principles of God's Word and teach them to our children early in life.

Verse 7 is a key verse in chapter 16: "When a man's ways please the Lord, he maketh even his enemies to be at peace with him." I think that the leaders of our nation would do well to internalize that verse. Why is America in such peril today? We have no promise that there will ever be a time when we do not have national enemies, but I am convinced that America is going through a time of struggle and trial because our ways—our thought life—are not pleasing to the Lord. Many bad things are happening, yet we seem to be giving such a low priority to them at high levels of our government. I think we can corporately say that when a nation's ways please the Lord, God will make even that nation's enemies to be at peace with that nation.

Another key verse is verse 18: "Pride goeth before destruction, and an haughty spirit before a fall." Pride is the threshold to ruin and destruction, and God hates a proud look. May God deliver us from pride, which springs from the way we think.

Pure Thoughts

Proverbs 16 divides into four parts. Verses 1-3 talk about the Christian's thought life. Is it possible to keep the mind clear of impurity? The answer to that is yes. Verse 3 says, "Commit thy works unto the Lord, and thy thoughts shall be established." If, as believers, we will internalize the commandments of God and commit ourselves to the lordship of Christ, we can have a total cleanup of all our thought processes, whether they are daydreams or night dreams.

Some people think they have no control over the terrible immoral dreams that capture their minds in daytime and at night. When you pillow your head at night, it is possible to keep the mind clear during the night. According to verse 13: "Commit thy works unto the Lord, and thy *thoughts* shall be established." Do you know why you sometimes dream bad things or think of shameful things when your mind rambles during the day? Likely you have been feeding bad things into your mind. "As he thinketh in his heart, so is he" (Prov. 23:7). Pollution that goes in through the eyes and the ears will corrupt the mind, the intellect, and the will. That is one reason I take such a strong stand against pornography.

Whether it is on the television screen, the movie screen, or the newsstand, it is still pornography. We do not need to read garbage. I often hear criticism that preachers are out to violate the First Amendment freedoms of the pornographers. But I do not believe the framers of the First Amendment meant to protect pornography.

These mind-polluters remind us that we have a knob on the television set that will turn it off. But that is not the idea. If I or my children go to the water spigot in my kitchen and turn it on, we have the right to believe that the water coming out of that spigot into the glass is safe to drink. It should not unexpectedly poison us. It comes from a public waterworks, and it is supposed to be kept safe for the public. The television airwaves are public and are owned by the people, not by the networks or by the FCC. The people have a right to know when they turn on the knob that what is coming into their living rooms is not poisonous to the moral values of their children and their families. If the networks want to do some knob-turning, let them turn it off at their own end before they dump their filth into our living rooms.

If you want your thoughts to be established and to have a pure mind, read the Word of God and fellowship with godly people. Stay away from people who tell dirty jokes, and do not tell them yourself. Do not read, watch, look at, or listen to that which is filthy. If you keep your eyes, your mind, and your heart clean, then when you are sleeping at night your dreams will be clean. Verses 1-3 of chapter 16 speak about the dreaming mind.

Now consider what Solomon says about the vain mind: "The Lord hath made all things for Himself: yes, even the wicked for the day of evil. Everyone that is proud in heart is an abomination to the Lord; though hand join in hand, he shall not be unpunished" (vv. 4-5).

What about thinking proud thoughts? What about the "I'll-do-as-I-please" attitude? What about the hedonist and the pleasure worshipers? What about those today who are materialistic? How many times have you read stories of people who have won a million dollars with lottery tickets and you wished you had that ticket? The world developed the crazy notion that somehow, sometime, you will be able to get something for nothing. Without working for it, you can still be wealthy. That is simply vain thinking, materialism, and it will ruin and wreck your life. You never get anything without paying the biblical price for it. "Everyone that is proud in heart is an abomination to the Lord; though hand join in hand, he shall not be unpunished" (v. 5).

What about pleasure? People get furious, for example, when we tell them that there are certain principles about the marriage bond. I was on a talk show from midnight to 3 A.M. with Larry King one night. The next day I went over to a one-hour show on a Washington television station. On both programs, people can call in. One caller asked who I thought I was to tell her she could not have an abortion if she wanted one. They call in and say they want freedom of choice—they will make their own decisions. I believe in freedom of choice too. But I believe the little baby should have a choice. What about those little babies? Somebody has got to speak for them; they cannot speak for themselves. Yet I believe the women who are pushing the proabortion position should have a choice too. But they ought to make the choice before life becomes a reality. They ought not to say, "I'll live as I please, do my own thing, and if a life comes into the picture, I'll destroy it." They will not do it—verse 5 tells us—without being punished. "Though hand join in hand" means that even if all the pornographers, abortionists, secular humanists, legislators, and even the Supreme Court say it is legal, offenders will not go unpunished.

I was reading about herpes in *Time* magazine. Twenty

million Americans have this incurable venereal disease. That is almost one in ten of our total population. Back in the '60s and '70s, the "do your own thing" of moral permissiveness was being taught. Homosexuals were coming out of the closets. We have seen the normalizing of what God has condemned as dirty and filthy—premarital sex, extramarital sex, and various live-in arrangements. *Time* magazine says herpes is called "Jerry Falwell's Revenge." That is actually the name they gave it. But in actuality, it is "God Almighty's Revenge," predicated on Galatians 6:7: "Be not deceived; God is not mocked, for whatsoever a man soweth, that shall he also reap." *Time* reports that the medical people and the social engineers are working furiously to find a drug to cure herpes. But that is not the answer. Stop the cause! We are breaking the Law of God. We are thinking vain thoughts when we try to violate all the principles of morality, with the idea that we can get by with it. That is a total impossibility, the product of the proud mind.

The Scheming Mind

Verses 8-17 form the third division of chapter 16. I like to call it "the scheming mind," because verse 9 says, "A man's heart deviseth his way, but the Lord directeth his steps." Man can scheme his way. In fact, verse 33 ties in with this: "The lot is cast into the lap, but the whole disposing thereof is of the Lord." God is in control of our lives. We sometimes get the crazy idea that we can be deceitful and dishonest—break the rules and be excused. Verse 11 says, "A just weight and balance are the Lord's." That means that God loves fairness in every business deal. Verse 12 points out that "it is an abomination to kings to commit wickedness, for the throne is established by righteousness." We cannot operate by conniving and scheming to circumvent the principles and Law of God and still come out with something good.

A good definition of *living by faith* is "living without scheming." We simply need to trust God, to love His Word, and to know what the Word says. We need to take all the commandments and the promises at face value and thus live without scheming. That is living by faith. God wants to capture that mind of yours so you are not thinking about how you are going to work out all your problems, or how you are going to do somebody in, or deceive somebody. God wants you to consider, rather, how you can be a blessing to others.

The Deceiving Mind

Finally, verses 19 through the end of the chapter comprise the fourth division. Here we have the deceiving mind. Several key verses explain the concept. Verse 19 says, "Better it is to be of an humble spirit with the lowly, than to divide the spoil with the proud." This is just another way of saying it is better to be poor and honest, than wealthy and dishonest.

Verse 25 is another key verse: "There is a way that seemeth right unto a man, but the end thereof are the ways of death." Whenever I am in a debate over salvation by grace through the shed blood of Jesus Christ, someone will invariably ask one particular question: "Do you believe that all people go to hell who do not believe the Gospel of Jesus Christ—the death, burial, and resurrection of the Son of God?" And I am sure they believe that, since we are usually on a massive radio or television network, or because there is a large local audience, I will sidestep the issue and say I do not believe that is literal. But the truth is that the Scriptures are clear on the matter. "He that hath the Son hath life; and he that hath not the Son of God hath not life" (1 John 5:12). That is an absolute. That is why we should be committed to world evangelization. Everyone needs to hear and believe the Gospel of Jesus Christ. There is no way to heaven except through the shed blood of the Son of God, and that has always been and always will be the Christian message.

But the deceiving mind makes you think you can work your way to heaven by joining a church, by being baptized in water, or whatever. Your mind will deceive you. Cultists today all deny the deity of Jesus Christ. We have the modern liberal theologians today who deny the inspiration and inerrancy of Scripture. And then we have the false religions all over the world that promote other ways and means of salvation.

Building Successful Relationships

God has placed us in a world full of people. We each live in several environments—family, home, neighborhood, business, school, nation, and world. We are to have healthy relationships in all of these environments. Proverbs 17 gives us the biblical prerequisites for building successful relationships. There are so many interpersonal relationships into which God brings us that we simply must have biblical guidance for them. We have special relationships inside the home that require divine guidance. We each experience leadership roles at times. We are related to society as well. And each of us is related to the ministry God has called us to perform. Proverbs 17 speaks of all these relationships.

The key verse in the chapter is verse 22: "A merry heart doeth good like a medicine, but a broken spirit drieth the bones." Through the years I have often said that you do not determine a man's greatness by his talent or by his wealth, as the world does, but rather by what it takes to discourage him. When the heart is happy and bubbling over, there is no question about it, that person feels good all over. He is able to face life. He is able to face challenges and new experiences.

● *Relationships at home*—Now consider what the biblical requirements are for healthy relationships in the home. Verse 1 says, "Better is a dry morsel, and quietness therewith, than an house full of sacrifices with strife." Another way of saying that is, "Eating burned toast in a house with peace, love, and communication is better than having prime rib in a house where arguments and strife are prevalent." In America today many families and homes are falling apart because they have never learned to love each other. The biblical basis for the family is this: The husband is to be submitted to the lordship of Jesus Christ. The wife, like the husband, is likewise to be submitted to the lordship of Jesus Christ and to be in submission to her husband. The children are to be submitted to the lordship of Jesus Christ and to be in obedience and submission to both parents. If you mix all that up with real love, each person loving the other, you have an unbeatable and wonderful relationship.

Verse 6 has more to say about building family relationships: "Children's children [grandchildren] are the crown of old men." Building a family on biblical principles so that your children and your children's children become your glory is a wonderful thing. Grandchildren are the crown of old men, "and the glory of children are their fathers." When grandparents revere grandchildren, children revere their parents in the same way. I looked up to my father. I thought he was the greatest man in the world. My children look up to me—that same way. That is why it is so important to be good parents, biblically committed Christian parents.

There is even more about the home in verse 25: "A foolish son is a grief to his father, and bitterness to her that bare him." This was discussed briefly in chapter 5 of this book. It is worth further comment. Nothing can break the heart of a parent like a wayward, rebellious child. Many young people are out in the world living in sin, moral impurity, perhaps hooked on drugs. They have an obligation to God to confess their sins, go back to their parents, and respect and obey them. We have an obligation to revere our parents, because that is the first commandment with promise. Those are some of the biblical requirements for home relationships.

● *Relationships as leaders*—Next, I want to mention the relationships of leadership. Everyone is a leader. Moms and dads are leaders in their families. You may be a leader in the plant, the office, or the business. If you are a student, you may be a leader in your school. We are trying to train leaders at Liberty Baptist College and Schools in Lynchburg, Virginia. What the world needs today is godly leadership—godly civic and political leaders.

Some time ago I had occasion to be proud of the governor of my state, Charles Robb. A man was scheduled to die in the gas chamber for a terrible crime he had committed—brutal murder. The governor was out of town and could have stayed away, but he returned home out of courage, duty, and responsibility. He could have been the hero of every liberal in the nation by staying that execution. But he allowed it to proceed. Capital punishment is biblical, of course. Genesis 9:6 commands it for murder, long before the Law of Moses. The Law in Exodus 21:12-17 and in other places confirms capital punishment. In accord with the Law, Romans 13:4 continues the injunction. Governor Robb did the hard thing but the right thing. I called the governor and congratulated him. He made me glad to be a citizen of the state of Virginia. If we had more of that kind of leadership in America, we could all sleep a little easier at night. You cannot tell me that capital punishment is not a deterrent. Of course it is. If all potential murderers in society today knew that they would be executed if they pulled the trigger—not five years from now, but soon—they would give a little more thought to it. I believe we need to pray for our leaders just as Paul said (1 Tim. 2:1-2).

What are the biblical requirements for leadership? Notice Proverbs 17:7: "Excellent speech becometh not a fool, much less do lying lips a prince." First of all, a leader must have integrity and character. Second, see verse 26: "Also to punish the just is not good, nor to strike princes for equity." That simply means that a leader must be fair. So one of the biblical requirements for proper relationships in leadership is fairness. We must not punish the just.

Not long ago, in the State of Nebraska, the State Board of Education punished twenty-two Christian schools because they were *Christian*. The pastors who administer these schools out of their churches would not submit to licensure by the state. Just as they would not permit their Sunday School to be licensed, they would not permit their Monday-through-Friday school to be licensed. They were willing to meet all the conditions of attendance, truancy, academic excellence, testing, and such. Leaders should never punish the just. If I were a citizen of Nebraska, I would not rest until I had straightened out that crowd in Lincoln.

Verses 27-28 say, "He that hath knowledge spareth his words, and a man of understanding is of an excellent spirit. Even a fool, when he holdeth his peace, is counted wise, and he that shutteth his lips is esteemed a man of understanding." A good leader learns how to keep his mouth shut. A good listener is educated more rapidly than a good talker. A good leader must be willing to listen to what others are saying, and in fairness apply just rulings in every situation. That should be true in your home, your business, your political place of leadership, and certainly true of you as a spiritual shepherd, Sunday School teacher, and leader.

● *Social relationships*—Let us look next at the biblical requirements for relationships in society. Consider verse 9, "He that covereth a transgression seeketh love, but he that repeateth a matter separateth very friends." Another way to say it is, "Love forgets failures." If you want to have a good relationship with people, learn how to forgive and forget.

Suppose God dealt with us the way we often deal with others. Someone might say, "You just do not know what I have been through."/"You do not know the pressure I have been under."/"You do not understand what my family has been up against."/"You cannot fathom how those people up the street have treated us."/"You do not know what this terrible ordeal did to us." The question really is whether you should forgive or hate. Think that over now. We have an obligation to love everybody in spite of what they say or do. The principle of divine love is that the one offended goes to the offender, not the reverse. The Scripture says if your brother has something against you, *you* go to him (Matt. 5:23-24). That means that you look up the person who has something against you, and *you* try to make peace.

The offended one should be the peacemaker, not the offender. That is the biblical requirement for good and healthy relationships in society. Love forgets.

Then Proverbs 17:10 says, "A reproof entereth more into a wise man than a hundred stripes into a fool." In other words, if you are going to properly relate to society, learn how to accept criticism. Learn how to be corrected. If you are a wise Christian, one sentence of reproof will do you more good than a hundred stripes will do a rebel. However, there are some people you cannot correct. There are some people who will never apologize and who can never be told they made a mistake because they will become furious.

Verse 12 says, "Let a bear robbed of her whelps [cubs] meet a man, rather than a fool in his folly." That means it is better to run into a bear who has just had her cubs taken away from her than to run into a fool who has been told he made a mistake. We need to learn how to relate to people. If we are going to have good societal relationships, we must learn to have a humble spirit.

"A man void of understanding striketh hands, and

becometh surety in the presence of his friend" (v. 18). We dealt with this earlier. Again, this means you should not sign a note for anybody unless you are willing to stand good for that loan with the thought that the debtor may be unable to pay you back.

● *Relationships in ministry*—Verse 3 says, "The fining pot [refining pot] is for silver, and the furnace for gold, but the Lord trieth the hearts." First of all, the Holy Spirit is constantly ministering to us, shaving off the dross and polishing the shaft. Remember that all of this is part of our maturing in Christ. Then verse 5 notes, "Whoso mocketh the poor reproacheth his Maker, and he that is glad at calamities shall not be unpunished." Learn to love people. Learn to love the materially poor as well as the spiritually poor.

We are not to look in contempt upon any violator of God's Law. We are to love people. Your ministry cannot be real if you do not truly love people. I am convinced more and more that we have a lot of preachers in this country who feel their ministry is just a job. They do not really love people. If you really love people, you will keep on keeping on, no matter what it costs you. Some preachers tell me that nobody appreciates what they are doing. Where in the Bible does God tell us that you are supposed to be appreciated for what you are doing? I am convinced that if a preacher is preaching what he ought to be preaching, and living the way he ought to be living, he would have a hard time even getting elected dogcatcher. If he takes a stand against sin and against riotious living in society, those people whose lifestyle is being criticized are going to be against him. But because he is a man of God, he loves them anyhow.

Loving people is a part of our responsibility. Jesus showed that love when, on the cross between two thieves, He died and said, "Father, forgive them, for they know not what they do" (Luke 23:34). They nailed Him to the tree, but He took the sins of the world on Himself. His blood paid for our sin debt forever, and we are the ones who nailed Him there. It was not just the Jews or the Romans; every person who ever lived helped drive the spikes into the hands of the Lord Jesus. Our sins put Him there, and He went there willingly and laid down His life and said with His last breath, "Father, forgive them, for they know not what they do." That is how we are to live with people.

Five Kinds of People

Proverbs 18 introduces us to five kinds of people. We are warned about the first four types, but we are to pattern ourselves after the fifth type. The key verse is the final verse of the chapter. It reads, "A man that hath friends must show himself friendly, and there is a friend that sticketh closer than a brother" (v. 24). The five types of men mentioned by Solomon are: (1) the *antisocial* man (vv. 1-5); (2) the *contentious* man (vv. 6-12); (3) the *judgmental* man (vv. 13-15); (4) the *selfish* man (vv. 16-21); and (5) the *friendly* man (vv. 22-24).

● Solomon says that the *antisocial man* in verses 1-5 has "separated himself" (v. 1). He behaves in such a manner as to alienate himself from those around him. He is not only unsociable, but he cares only about his own selfish concerns. He criticizes others but has no plan of his own. The antisocial man has trouble because we live in a world of people. God has placed us here. Someone has said that God first saves us *out* of the world and then sends us back *into* the world to represent Him to the world. God has not called us to be hermits.

A church looking for a new pastor required that he be a "good mixer." Well, that is not necessarily what this is speaking about. A man could be a good socializer, but by being wrong on doctrine could ruin a church. On the other hand, a person could have good doctrine, a clear understanding of the Word of God, and be completely true to Scripture; but by not loving people he could still ruin the church. So what really is needed when you are looking for a pastor is one who loves and believes the Word of God, but also loves people. That horizontal relationship is what Solomon is talking about in the first five verses of Proverbs 18. If we are going to be effective as parents, pastors, Sunday School teachers, and members of our community and the society in which we live, there are some requirements. We must love and believe the Word of God, be in love with Jesus Christ— but beyond that—we must also have a genuine love for people.

We have a real problem in our world today. The world is full of hate. We have blacks and whites hating each other, reds against yellows, Jews against Arabs, and Arabs against Jews. You do not have to go north and south in the United States. You can go anywhere in the world and find prejudice, racial hatred, and nationalism. These things have nothing to do with the color of the skin. It has to do with the sin in men's hearts, and the problem cannot be cured by education. It takes regeneration!

I can tell you how the prejudice got out of my heart. I met the Lord at eighteen in 1952 under the radio ministry of Charles E. Fuller, and God put His Holy Spirit in me, giving me a baptism of divine love. Only in Christ can you love all men unselfishly. I would challenge you with the thought that one day you are going to stand before Christ, "whom having not seen, ye love" (1 Peter 1:8). If we are to love our Saviour, whom we have never seen, God is certainly going to hold us accountable for whether or not we love people down here. "We know that we have passed from death unto life, because we love the brethren" (1 John 3:14). Let us not be antisocial people.

There are people perhaps on your street, on the very block where you live, who are filled with bitterness and hatred toward others. I sometimes meet members of families who have not spoken for years. There is certainly nothing Christian about that. If you are going to be successful, you must learn to love not only God but people as well. There will be those who wrong you and those who do not like you and some who will love you. God has determined to put you in situations where you can *learn* to be sociable. Have you ever noticed that many married couples with solid relationships are quite opposite in personality? Often the couples who really have it together are dispositional opposites. They relate to different things in different ways. They have different likes and dislikes, but they have learned in the Spirit of God to love and accept one another as they are and to go on serving God together as a team.

Now you may wonder why God put you in your job, to work alongside of an "old horned toad" nobody can get along with. God put you there to polish your personality. Do not be one who always says, "I have just got to find another job. I cannot work with this crowd—they're a bunch of heathen." God may have put you among those heathen for you to learn how not to be a heathen yourself, and to learn how to love people. God has set the example. "God so loved the world, that He gave His only begotten Son" (John 3:16), and while we were yet His enemies, God loved us and sent His Son to die for us. There is no excuse for anyone not loving people. All through my life I have maintained the philosophy that, if given a fair chance, I can get along with anybody. Now that position is tested very sorely these days when I take a position on issues like abortion, pronography, the traditional family, and secular humanism. There are some out there who literally hate those who take a stand for God. Just write a letter to the editor taking a strong biblical stand against some moral evil, sign your name, and see how many complimentary letters come in for you. We are to love the Norman Lears and the ACLU. Now, that does not mean we have to like what they do, but we love them in spite of the wrongdoing in which we feel they are involved.

● The *contentious man* is treated in verses 6-12. Verse 6 says, "A fool's lips enter into contention, and his mouth calleth for strokes." The mouth of the fool continually causes contention and calls for the strokes of justice. Worse than that is the fact that his mouth will eventually cause his destruction if not brought under control (v. 7). The contentious man is filled with pride, arrogance, and the bitter spirit of the antisocial man. He allows all this to produce an overflowing verbiage that is damaging to the character of others. You do not have to pull the trigger on a man to destroy his character. You can assassinate him with your tongue, and that is why Scripture deals so harshly with the busybody. Scripture speaks very strongly against gossip and malicious conversation that hurts and injures other people.

There are three golden gates through which every word about others should pass before we speak those words:

First, is it true? Is it absolutely, irrevocably *true*? Do you know it is true?

Second, if it is true, do we *need* to say it? Some things which are true do not need to be repeated.

Third, if it is true and needful, is it *kind*? Is that statement you are going to make *kind* to others? If it is not true, needful, and kind, you need to close your lips tightly before the words escape. Once the words are out of your mouth you cannot retrieve them. You can apologize; you can ask forgiveness, but the words are out and can never be recaptured.

Verse 12 says, "Before destruction the heart of man is haughty, and before honor is humility." Simply stated, pride produces ruin, and humility produces honor. I think you can decide which is the better. We need to be humble before others and never contentious about others.

• The third type of person mentioned in Proverbs 18 is the *judgmental man* in verses 13-15: "He that answereth a matter before he heareth it, it is folly and shame unto him. The spirit of a man will sustain his infirmity, but a wounded spirit who can bear? The heart of the prudent getteth knowledge, and the ear of the wise seeketh knowledge." Thus, when all the evidence is in, one's previous accusations or conclusions may be proven false. Jesus said, "Judge not, that ye be not judged" (Matt. 7:1). We are to be discerning but not judgmental. The judgmental man is playing God. He believes he knows what is in the heart of the other individual when only God can know that.

I am often asked if someone or other is saved. I cannot answer. I do not know what is in the person's heart. There are some attitudes and actions that might indicate that he is or is not, but I cannot know for sure whether he is saved. Only God knows that, and you and I need to have that attitude toward everybody. God alone is the judge.

• Fourth, consider the *selfish man* in verses 16-21: "A man's gift maketh room for him, and bringeth him before great men. He that is first in his own cause seemeth just, but his neighbor cometh and searcheth him." The selfish man is thinking only of what benefits him. He asks, "How much will I make?"/"What do I get out of this?"/"What is the bottom line for me?" The unselfish person who is Christ-filled and in love with people is thinking just the opposite. When looking at a situation, the unselfish person always wants to know all sides. He is not the judgmental person or the contentious person or the antisocial man. Instead, the wise and unselfish Christian is looking at how he can be a blessing to others. He wants to know what he can do for others, and in the process, how he can bring honor and glory to God.

● Finally, look at the *friendly man* in verses 22-24. Verse 24 says, "A man that hath friends must show himself friendly, and there is a friend that sticketh closer than a brother." One's acquisition of friends is directly dependent on his ability to demonstrate friendliness toward others. The friend that "sticketh closer than a brother" refers to our Lord Jesus Christ who is the Friend of every believer and the Friend of sinners. He will never desert us.

The friendly man, first of all, is able to establish a godly, healthy home. The friendly man makes a good husband because he is not antisocial, contentious, judgmental, or selfish. The friendly woman makes a good wife.

To have a good family there must be love and understanding and kindness. Verse 24 tells us that in order for other people to appreciate and love you as a friend, you must show yourself friendly. I get letters occasionally from people who say, "I visited a church the other day, and nobody shook my hand." The first question I always have in my mind is, "Did you approach anybody to shake his hand?" Friendliness is created. When I walk into a room, I do not stand and wait for everybody to come and greet me. I begin looking for people. If they do not care to shake hands, they will have to turn me down, because I am going to try. When I am driving along the highway, I wave at people. I do not know all of them and cannot see half of them, but I just wave.

I waved at a fellow driving a beer truck one day, and he parked his beer truck that afternoon and quit his job. He came to church the next Sunday and got saved—then came to college and trained to be a preacher. His name is Tim Setliff, and he now pastors a church in Lynchburg, Virginia.

Friendliness is contagious. You ought to spread the germ. You ought to be the one looking for somebody to spread love and friendliness with. Be friendly. Be the kind of individual God desires you to be.

8

Accentuating the Positive
Proverbs 19—21

Columnist Ann Landers once reported that she receives about 10,000 letters each month from people seeking advice. Asked what problem tops the list, her reply was that most people were afraid of something. They were afraid of losing health, wealth, and loved ones. They were actually afraid of life itself. An attitude of fear will control one's responses to the situations of life. Peter declared that "God hath not given us the spirit of fear, but of power, and of love, and of a sound mind" (2 Tim. 1:7). We can and must have the proper attitudes to live successfully.

In all of life, we need to accentuate the positives while avoiding the negatives. Proverbs 19 deals with developing the proper attitudes basic to living. Without proper attitudes toward the various challenges we meet in life, we will be failures.

Five Attitudes That Affect Our Lives
Chapter 19 speaks of attitudes that affect five areas of our lives.

● *Business*—First of all, in verses 1-5, Solomon mentions that we need to develop a proper attitude toward business. I am not speaking only about the businessman. We are all involved in business, if nothing more than in providing for personal needs and the needs of our families.

Our attitude is very important. Every one of us does something wrong every day, and 1 John 1:9 says, "If we confess our sins, He [God] is faithful and just to forgive us our sins, and to cleanse us from all unrighteousness." The dean of students at Liberty Baptist College can tell you that dealing with students over breaking rules is not a difficult thing if those young people realize they have done wrong and say from a sincere heart that they would like another chance. We have no problem working with young people who have this attitude. But our dean would also tell you that when a student has a bad attitude and refuses to humble himself or herself, then—no matter what the situation, small or great— that attitude is destructive. It is almost impossible to deal with.

In this country, we have attitude problems. We have people who are trying to tear down business and the free enterprise system. We have people teaching in public and state universities who are avowed Marxist-Leninists and against the free enterprise system. Read what the Word of God says about business. God is in favor of freedom, property ownership, competition, diligence, work, and acquisition. All of this is taught in the Word of God in both the Old and New Testaments.

Proverbs 19:1 says, "Better is the poor that walketh in his integrity, than he that is perverse in his lips, and is a fool." This means it is better to be poor and honest than wealthy and dishonest. The basic cornerstone for your activities in business should be integrity or honesty. Everything you say must be true. That does not mean that you will not make mistakes. That does not mean you will not have financial reverses. But it means that you are always honest, and that whatever you say is so, to the best of your knowledge. Now in our country today that is not always the premise, but if we as Christians are going to be successful and have the blessing of God on our business lives, we must have the attitude that honesty is the only way. It is not the best policy; it is the only policy.

Then verse 5 adds, "A false witness shall not be unpunished, and he that speaketh lies shall not escape." If we are going to be successful in business, we must be honest. The reason the United States can never get anywhere with the Soviet Union in treaties, contracts, and other agreements is that the Soviet government is not trustworthy. They have one goal, and that is world conquest. Their leaders will say anything at any time to accomplish their goal. When you deal with dishonest people you cannot win.

● *Government*—Second, verses 6-10 speak of developing proper attitudes toward government. Verse 6 says, "Many will entreat the favor of the prince, and every man is a friend to him that giveth gifts." God has ordained government. The Scripture tells us that "the powers that be are ordained of God" (Rom. 13:1). Congressmen have a high calling. Romans 13 suggests that congressmen are ministers of God. They are called of God into that position just as much as I am called to the pulpit. Government and power are not supposed to be the same thing. Government is the God-ordained entity by which societies ae regulated, protected, and kept civilized. They protect and guard the rights of individuals, and we should respect our leaders. I do not agree with all the members of Congress, but I respect the position they fill. They have my respect and my prayers (1 Tim. 2:1-2).

● *Family*—Third, we need to develop proper attitudes toward the family, according to verses 11-16. Verse 11 says,

"The discretion of a man deferreth his anger, and it is his glory to pass over a transgression." What does that mean? In the family you can either see a lot of things that are not right, or you can prefer to overlook a few things. Parents, your children do not need to be bawled out constantly for every little accident. Learn to help your children up, not down. Do you know why a lot of young people leave home as quickly as possible? Perhaps to get away from a hardheaded, fussing, grouchy parent. But then they often marry somebody they did not really want to marry, but it seemed a privilege just to get away. Some parents are so legalistic that their boys and girls feel they cannot do anything right.

Nothing ruins a boy or girl as much as a morally permissive home, unless it is an overly legalistic home. You need to give some liberty and some leeway without being too permissive. This mean spirit that many parents have makes their children grow up to hate them.

Solomon, again, has a word for children in verse 13, "A foolish son is the calamity of his father." This refers to a *rebellious* son, as previously discussed. Children, obey your parents. Do not rebel. Your parents are ordained of God to be your superiors. Dad and Mom may not always be right, but they are always in charge. You have an obligation to God to obey your parents.

Now, there is a third point here. Verse 13 mentions "the contentions of a wife." The arguments of a wife "are a continual dropping [dripping]." Drip, drip, drip. Were you ever in a house where you have turned the faucet off as far as it will go, and it still drips and drives you nuts? That is what Solomon says a nagging woman will do for you: nag, nag, nag.

Solomon is quite practical. He started off with husbands. We had it coming first. Husbands, love your family and your children. Do not be negative, critical, and legalistic. Do not keep telling them what their faults are. Tell them what is right with them. Mom, quit your nagging and be as sweet as you can. When Dad gets home from a hard day's work, try not to meet him at the door with a rundown of the day's problems. Say something sweet to him when he walks in. Let him know that home is the best place on earth to be. If Mom and Dad practice that, and the kids follow this principle, they can have a sweet, loving Christian home. There may be a lot of mistakes in the home, but the verse says the glory of a discerning man is to pass over some of those things and to help the family.

● *The poor*—The fourth point of chapter 19 is developing a proper attitude toward the poor. "He that hath pity upon the poor lendeth unto the Lord, and that which he hath given will He pay him again" (v. 17). This is fantastic. Solomon said that giving money to the poor—those who have less than you do—is really making a loan to the Lord. And, believe me, God is a good credit risk. Not only will He pay back the principal, but He also pays the highest interest in town.

I believe in storehouse tithing. I teach it, preach it, and practice it. But almost daily God brings all of us in contact with people who have great needs. Do you know what you are doing when you help meet the needs of the poor? You are lending to the Lord. You are actually putting it in the hand of God rather than in the poor man's hand. And He will give it back to you with interest. If you have not learned that yet, you need to learn it. Do not be arrogant and proud over what you have. There is nothing wrong with having things, as long as things do not have you. Remember that you are the trustee, not the owner. God is the owner and you are just the steward. May God help us develop a proper attitude toward the poor.

● *Personal habits*—The final section of chapter 19 deals with developing proper attitudes toward our personal habits (vv. 18-29). Let me briefly mention a number of important areas under this heading. Verse 18 says, "Chasten thy son while there is hope, and let not thy soul spare for his crying." Disciplining my children is difficult for me, but it is necessary. If you love your children, you will punish them at times.

Second, verse 19 reads, "A man of great wrath shall suffer punishment, for if thou deliver him, yet thou must do it again." Get the victory over an uncontrollable temper. There is nothing worse than a man who is a time bomb, always blowing his stack and yelling and being unkind to people.

Verse 20 says, "Hear counsel." Learn how to take advice. Do not be so proud and mighty that nobody can tell you anything. Learn to listen to others.

Another point regarding personal habits is found in verse 21: "There are many devices in a man's heart; nevertheless, the counsel of the Lord, that shall stand." Man proposes but God disposes. You can make all your plans and do all your work, but God Almighty adds it up and brings out the final conclusion.

There is something else in verse 24. "A slothful man hideth his hand in his bosom, and will not so much as bring it to his mouth again." There are some people so lazy they will not reach down with a fork to get a piece of food to put in their mouths. They want you to put it in their mouths for them. God is against slothfulness and laziness.

Lastly, look at verse 26: "He that wasteth [abuses] his father, and chaseth away his mother, is a son that causeth shame." Always respect your parents. Do not ever, ever, ever disrespect your parents. That is the first commandment with promise. God said that He will prolong our days on the earth if we respect our parents.

Be an Instrument of Blessing

We have seen what proper attitudes toward life should be. God has given us in Proverbs 19 a plan for becoming sweet, overcoming, positive Christians in our attitudes toward every area of life. God does not want us to be negative, cynical, defeated, bitter, malicious. God wants us to be positive, loving, kind, gracious. He wants us to be instruments of blessing to others. That is just what God did in His Son Jesus 2,000 years ago when perfect God and perfect Man merged as one personality.

Eight Areas to Shun

Besides developing proper attitudes in many areas of our lives, there are some things we simply need to avoid. There are eight taboos in chapter 20 that Christians should shun. Before considering these eight prohibitions, let's look at two key verses in the chapter.

Verse 27 is a key verse: "The spirit of man is the candle of the Lord, searching all the inward parts of the belly." That could be translated this way: "The conscience of man is the spotlight of the Holy Spirit that makes us feel bad when we do wrong." Thank God for that truth. God has put into human beings that thing we call a conscience. It is called here "the spirit of man" and "the candle of the Lord." When you say something you should not have said, or do something you should not have done, if you are a spiritual person you feel bad right away. You will not feel better until you go to that person you have wronged and make it right, and until you go to God and make it right. That is our human conscience. May God deliver us from becoming like some who are described in Romans 1 as being past conscience, or whose conscience has been seared. They have violated every Law of God so often that they feel bad about nothing. Militant homosexuals are listed that way in Romans 1, and Paul says that God gives them over to a reprobate mind because of it.

Then verse 29 contains another key idea: "The glory of young men is their strength, and the beauty of old men is the gray head." One commentator has said it this way: "The glory of young men is their strength while the glory of old men is their experience." A wise businessman knows that in any successful enterprise you need young, aggressive, never-say-no men and women, but you must also have stable, solid, older people with experience, who will not allow drastic and tragic errors. An athletic team is that way. Thank God for these young athletes who do not know any better than to run into a linebacker head-on standing up. But thank God for an older man who, when the team is falling apart, can be a team leader and pull the team back together and keep it from collapsing. We need both. That is true in the church also. I pastor a fairly young church, but I am thankful for the old-timers who helped start it, because every time we start getting a little too exuberant and energetic they will very graciously come by and say, "Pastor, I think maybe we'd better look at that one more time." Gray hair can teach things you cannot learn in a classroom.

Now, let me point out in chapter 20 the things we need to shun.

● *Strong drink*—Solomon wrote, "Wine is a mocker, strong drink is raging, and whosoever is deceived thereby is not wise" (v. 1). I am amazed at how the Madison Avenue crowd and the television industry and the liquor trade try to give the macho image to the fellow who is hooked on booze. That superstar athlete performs all during his athletic career without liquor because he could not be the superstar if he were addicted to it. But as soon as he retires, things change. He is not getting that big paycheck anymore, so here comes one brewery after another, saying, "Hey, you need to work for us. We can pay you a lot of money." Suddenly, they are sitting around a table telling young impressionable minds how desirable a certain brand of liquor is. There is nothing macho about drinking alcoholic beverages. I do not believe a man is bad because he drinks, but I believe he would be a better man if he did not drink.

You say, "Can I go to heaven as a social drinker?" I think you can go to heaven doing a lot of things you ought not to do, but that is not the issue. The issue is, do you want to be the maximum for Christ? I think you do. Business leaders make a mistake, I think, when they have their conventions. They have got to have one big drunken party night. That is unnecessary. Businessmen should be able to have a convention for three or four days and nights and work, learn, fellowship, and have a great time without having a drunken party. I think they would learn more and come home more edified.

Let me give a personal example. My father was fifty-five years of age when he died. There never was a daddy who loved his children any more than my dad did. He provided well for us, and we never had a moment of want in all of our lives. I was fifteen years old when Dad died. I was standing by his bed, holding his hand, October 10, 1948. He was one of those fellows who said, "I can handle mine." I never saw Daddy really drunk. He could always work hard, run the business, go to bed late, and get up early, but he drank every day. Finally, my father, whom I loved very much, contracted cirrhosis of the liver and died a relatively young man, depriving his children of a daddy. I do not know when I will die, but when I do I hope it will not be because I was undisciplined or violated some of God's principles.

Addiction to strong drink is a violation. You do not need it in your life. I became an archenemy of alcoholic beverages when I saw what it did to my dad. If no booze problems existed in this country, there would be a lot of empty cells in our prisons. And many of the thousands who die each year on our highways would still be alive. Liquor is a bad business.

• *Civil disobedience*—The second taboo is found in verse

2: "The fear of a king is as the roaring of a lion, whoso provoketh him to anger sinneth against his own soul." This is disobedience to civil law. We should teach our sons and daughters to respect police officers. They represent civil law—"the powers that be are ordained of God" (Rom. 13:1). We should teach children to respect members of the armed forces, because they too are representative of civil law and civil government. Back during the '60s and '70s universities were throwing ROTC units off the campuses. Now they are begging them to come back. The only time you and I have any right to violate the law of man is when the law of man tells us to violate the Law of God. That is not too often either, especially in this country.

● *Work*—Our third area of prohibition is found in verse 4: "The sluggard [lazy man] will not plow by reason of the cold; therefore shall he beg in harvest, and have nothing." This refers to the rejection of the work ethic. This nation was formed by men and women who carved it out of the wilderness. They worked six-day weeks, twelve-hour days. Today we want something for nothing. May God help us teach our sons and daughters to obey the work ethic.

● *Dishonesty*—God has another area for us to shun: "Divers weights, and divers measures [the modern way is having two sets of books], both of them are alike abomination to the Lord" (v. 10). I call this dishonesty in business. Whether it is dishonesty toward your government by not paying the taxes you should pay or dishonesty to your employer by taking long coffee breaks, honesty in business should be a way of life for a Christian.

● *Unsecured loans*—There is another taboo in verse 16: "Take his garment that is surety for a stranger, and take a pledge for him for a strange woman." This is lending without collateral. The Word of God—according to this verse and others already noted in previous lessons—orders us not to endorse someone else's note unless three things are true. I mentioned them earlier. I do not need the money myself; losing it will not affect my family; and I will still love the man even if I have to pay off his note. That is what the Word of God says. The best way to make an enemy is to sign his note. Our country, by the way, has learned that in our foreign aid program. You cannot buy friends.

● *Gossip*—The sixth taboo is participation in gossip. "He that goeth about as a talebearer revealeth secrets; therefore meddle not with him that flattereth with his lips" (v. 19). The old-timers used to say of a talebearer, "The person who will bring a bone will also carry one." We need victory in this area of our lives. Do not say anything to anybody anywhere about another person that you could not lovingly and graciously say to the person himself. If you practice that principle, you will be a great blessing to others, and your example may encourage others to follow suit.

● *Disrespect for parents*—The seventh prohibition to heed in chapter 20 is that of disrespect for parents. Verse 20 says, "Whoso curseth his father or his mother, his lamp shall be put out in obscure darkness." That means that God will abbreviate your life. Did you know that no matter what your Mom and Dad have done to you—no matter how unkind, how unthoughtful they have been—you never have a right to disrespect them? Bitterness toward your parents is forbidden by the Word of God. Even if your mother was a prostitute and your daddy is in prison, you are supposed to respect, love, and pray for them—no matter what they have done to you. That is the first commandment with promise. God said obey, respect, honor, and revere your parents. If you do, your days will be long on the earth (Ex. 20:12). If you respect your parents, God will lengthen your days, but it also says there that if you disrespect your parents, God will cut your days short. Do you want to live a long time? I do. I never raised my voice to my mother or my daddy in all of my life. I thank God I can say that before Him and the holy angels, and I hope you feel that way too. As mentioned, my father had a drinking problem, but I never turned against him.

● *Vengeance*—Finally, look at the eighth area to shun— taking vengeance against enemies. Verse 22 warns, "Say not thou, I will recompense evil, but wait on the Lord, and He shall save thee." God says, "Do not try to retaliate. If your enemies do something to you, love them." Leave the whole matter in the Lord's hands. You know, God can work out these situations so much better than you can. In my thirty years as a Christian how many times God has dealt with my enemies without my intervening except to pray for them. If you will leave it in the hands of the Lord, God will work it out. God will vindicate you if your heart is right. You do not have to become vicious like your enemies. In meekness and quietness of spirit, leave with the Lord your anxieties over those who hate you. He can do a much better job than you or I can possibly imagine.

God's Sovereignty in Man's Affairs
God is going to have His way in the affairs of men. He is sovereign. I believe Proverbs 21 speaks of God's sovereignty in five different areas. God is in control in (1) the affairs of government (v. 1); (2) the affairs of the poor (v. 13); (3) the affairs of the pleasure-seekers (v. 17); (4) the affairs of the wicked (v. 18); and in (5) the affairs of war (v. 31).

Knowing that God really is in control is a consoling thought. There is a tendency today to think that the world is out of control, that God is no longer on the throne, and that things are going awry everywhere. There are crises too numerous to name, and horrible events are happening all over the world today. Even the news media can hardly keep up with all the earthquakes, hijackings, famines, wars, economic collapses, and other frightening occurrences.

God Controls Government

God tells us that He is in control of every area. First of all, He is in control of governments. Verse 1 says, "The king's heart is in the hand of the Lord, as the rivers of water; He turneth it whithersoever He will." But, for example, does God actually rule in the affairs of the American government? We have many politicians who do not know God. There are many unjust and inequitable things going on in Washington and in the fifty state capitals. Can we believe that God has anything to do with American government? Look again at verse 1. It says, "The king's heart." Now, for us the "king" would be the President, the 100 senators, the 435 congressmen, the 50 governors, and many more state, county, and municipal officials.

Now you may ask whether it is possible that God could be in that, when most of those hundreds of people just mentioned are not Christians. That has nothing to do with it. "The king's heart is in the hand of the Lord." It does not matter who the king is. Later in this chapter, I will deal with Russia, but let us look at the United States right now. "The king's heart is in the hand of the Lord, as the rivers of water; He turneth it whithersoever He will." That means that when we pray, as we are instructed to do (1 Tim. 2:1-2), for the king and for all who are in authority—the President, the congressmen, the judges, the leaders of the nation—we put pressure on God through intercession. Remember that Christ is the King of kings and the Lord of lords; He is our Mediator. If you would like to get in touch with the President, get on your knees before God today or tonight and talk to God Almighty, and He will talk to the President.

Now I am happy we have a President who professes to be a Christian. Of course he is not perfect—nor is this preacher, nor are you. Some time ago I ate with the President and others. He gave a ten-minute address that I wish all Americans could have heard. It was really a call for spiritual awakening in America. As I was sitting there, I had a hard time not shouting "Hallelujah!" But whether a President is a Christian or not has nothing to do with his heart being in the hand of the Lord.

Let us skip over the water to Moscow. Nobody has ever accused any Russian leader of being a Christian. Yet the heart of the present head of the USSR is in the hand of the Lord. That is exactly what the text says. It does not matter who he is. "The king's heart is in the hand of the Lord." Chernenko does not know it, but God knows it, and you know it, and if you will talk to God, God will take care of it. God can wake him up like He did Nebuchadnezzar or Belshazzar. He can wake him up in the night. He could want to go *this* way, and God could send him *that* way. We need to pray for leaders so we can have a peaceful environment and make Christ known to others.

God Rules in Affairs of the Poor

Second, God rules in the affairs of the poor. "Whoso stoppeth his ears at the cry of the poor, he also shall cry himself, but shall not be heard" (v. 13). I have been to Cambodia, Thailand, and many other parts of the world where the mothers do not have milk to give their little babies before they go to bed or when they get up the next morning. Millions through the years have died of malnutrition and starvation. Is God not aware of all that? Does God not know where the poor are? I tell you that God does know and that God pleads for the poor. He is the Advocate of the poor. He is the Advocate of the underdog. He is the Advocate of the person who has no advocate on this earth; and if you want the blessing of God in your life, open your ears to the cry of the poor. Somewhere in your life today, God will bring you into contact with somebody who needs something desperately, and God may give you that wonderful privilege of opening your ear and extending your hand and being blessed of heaven because of it. There is a sovereignty in the dealings of men with the poor. "He that hath pity upon the poor lendeth unto the Lord" (19:17). That is what Solomon said. When you give to the poor you are making a loan to God, and He pays good interest and has never defaulted.

God Rules the Pleasure Seekers
Third, notice that God rules and is sovereign in the affairs of the hedonists, the pleasure seekers, and worshipers of false gods. "He that loveth pleasure shall be a poor man; he that loveth wine and oil shall not be rich" (v. 17). He who lives high will wind up in poverty. He who loves pleasure shall be poor.

America is right now in the throes of several epidemics. We have a drug epidemic that, in my opinion, is nothing more than the judgment of God on a nation that shut God out of the public schools twenty years ago. God is light. When light is absent, the natural sequel is darkness. The drug epidemic is part of the darkness that is destroying the minds, bodies, and lives of the children in our schools today.

Then, as mentioned, there is the herpes epidemic raging in our country. I believe that God is judging America because of moral permissiveness. On one television program I saw, several people who had herpes were on the show actually saying they would now have to be more careful about their promiscuity and more selective in their immorality, instead of saying, that they should stop doing what they have been doing. The only way to cure the herpes problem is for people to quit breaking God's Law relating to sex.

Why cannot somebody on television, perhaps a talk-show

host—somebody other than preachers—say that God intended marriage to be one man for one woman? And God did not call us to be animals. He called us to be human beings with moral values, and there is not a verse in the Bible that condones extramarital and premarital sex. But there are hundreds of verses that condemn it! America is getting away from that. There is only one thing we can do, and that is to have a spiritual awakening so the next generation will not reap our whirlwind.

Why are we experiencing a conservative sweep today, morally, politically, and socially? It is quite simple: the young people of our country are too smart to fall into the same trap their parents did. They are repudiating the chaos of their parents' young lives. As the Gallup Poll put it, the children are more conservative than the parents today. I believe with all my heart that the country is going to have a spiritual and a moral awakening in the 1980s. May God Almighty help us as a country to get back to moral decency and come back to those values that count!

God Rules the Wicked

Next, consider verse 18: "The wicked shall be a ransom for the righteous, and the transgressor for the upright." This expresses the sovereignty of God in the affairs of the wicked. Did you ever feel like the ungodly are prospering, and the godly are suffering? Like the ungodly are profiting and the godly are hurting? Did you ever stop to think that something is not fair about all this? Did you ever complain in your heart about how So-and-so seems to have no problems, gets along beautifully, with everything going his way, while he is violating every Law of God? Yet you are trying to live for God, and everything seems to be going wrong. Of course you have felt that way at times. We all have. But we must not forget that Saturday or next year is not always payday on God's calendar.

He does not pay annually, but He always pays. He keeps immaculate books. He has never made a mathematical error in His books. The Bible says, "Whatsoever a man soweth, that shall he also reap" (Gal. 6:7). In another place, Jesus said, "For what shall it profit a man, if he gain the whole world, and lose his own soul?" (Mark 8:36)

There are so many atrocities happening around the world today. The Communists—since the Bolshevik Revolution in 1917—have murdered 142 million people. Now that is quite a group to be murdered. When several hundred were murdered by the Lebanese in one of their refugee camps some years ago during the Israeli occupation, everyone was yelling for withdrawal of Israeli troops and resignation of Israeli leaders. When Lt. William Calley massacred a group of civilians in Vietnam, no one called for our President to resign. Why? What was the difference? There is a great deal of anti-Semitism in our world today. But may we be mindful that God is keeping the books and when He balances them, the just will come out all right, but the wicked will not.

And Even in Affairs of War

Finally, there is the sovereignty of God in the affairs of war. Verse 31 says, "The horse is prepared against the day of battle, but safety is of the Lord." You can prepare yourself for the conflict: "but safety is of the Lord." Only God can give the victory. Everybody is afraid of nuclear war. I wish there had never been a nuclear bomb. I wish we could go back to the other side of 1945 and blot the nuclear bomb out of history, but we cannot do that. We do not have any idea how many nations have the bomb. The situation is out of control. The question is, "How can I sleep? What in the world are we going to do?" I believe in peace negotiations. I believe in doing everything we can for peace. Scripture says we should live peaceably with all men as far as possible (Rom. 12:18).

That means we should go to the nth degree to try to accomplish peace, but at the same time, as a child of God, I can go to bed every night knowing that even the affairs of war are in the hands of the Lord.

When the fathers of our nation could not agree on a constitution, Ben Franklin, never accused of being a Fundamentalist, stood and said, "Sirs, I've lived a long time, and the longer I live the more convincing proof I see of this truth: God rules in the affairs of men, and if a sparrow cannot fall to the ground without His notice, is it probable that an empire can rise without His aid?" He called the convention to prayer, and the result was that magnificent Constitution on which the United States is based. He reminded them that during the war with Britain they had prayed in that very chamber, and God supernaturally took a tiny poverty-ridden colony and helped its colonists defeat the great British empire. Then he asked the question of the convention: "Have we now forgotten the powerful Friend?"

And the question I would ask today is, "Have you forgotten that powerful Friend?" We should do all we can for the cause of peace. We should do all we can to defend our nation. But at the same time we need to look up and say, "Lord, it is all in Your hands—even the affairs of war. I am going to bed tonight and get eight hours of good sleep, and I will trust You to take care of it."

There are no panic buttons near the throne. God does not have high blood pressure. Everything is under control, and you can trust God to take care of you, your family, and your nation if you are meeting His conditions. He is sovereign in the affairs of government, in the affairs of the poor, the hedonists, the wicked, and in the affairs of war. We can trust God.

9

God's Perspective on Man's World

Proverbs 22—24

Before man can place proper value on the things of life, he needs to have means to measure value. God's perspective on man's world, therefore, is all-important. How does God view the events of my life? How will He evaluate my life and conduct at the Judgment Seat? Have I accomplished anything for eternity? Are my goals in line with His? Are my methods and motives in accord with those of the Almighty? Do I view things from His perspective? These are some of the matters Solomon talks about in Proverbs 22—24.

Man's Need for Credibility

First, Proverbs 22 emphasizes the need we have for building credibility in all our relationships. All of life involving the development of character should be aimed at the goal of building credibility. If people cannot believe in you, it really does not matter how well you say something. If your word is worthless, or your character is flawed, it really does not matter how much you accomplish or accumulate in life. I am grateful for those people who have lived and died and left behind a heritage of character, integrity, love, compassion, and decency. Few things are more important than building credibility before our fellowmen. Of course, our credibility with God is most important, but it is also important that we have a horizontal relationship that makes the value of our ministry and life worthwhile.

● *"A good name"*—The first verse of chapter 22 begins with three words, "A good name." That is where the word *credibility* comes from. These first few verses speak about the acquiring of a good name and building credibility, first, by your personal relationships. We must get our priorities right, and in verse 1 we are told that "a good name is rather to be chosen than great riches, and loving favor rather than silver and gold." In a materialistic society, it is important to understand what we read in the New Testament. "A man's life consisteth not in the abundance of the things which he possesseth" (Luke 12:15). Paul said that we came into the world absolutely void of anything, and we will go out the same way (1 Tim. 6:7).

● *Priorities*—It is important to develop the proper priorities, and the first great priority is a personal relationship with God through Jesus Christ. Right behind your relationship with God Almighty should be your relationship with your family. I have an obligation to my wife, Macel, and our three children, Jerry, Jeannie, and Jonathan, that supersedes my responsibility to anyone else on earth. I am glad to be a pastor, but my ministry is third, behind my commitments to God and my family. Dr. Clyde Narramore said, "For what shall it profit a man if he save the whole world and lose his own children?" We have an obligation to God first, to our families second, and then, third, to our work, ministry, or vocation.

● *Philosophy*—The second word relating to developing personal relationships and building credibility is *philosophy.* Verse 2 says, "The rich and poor meet together; the Lord is the maker of them all." As far as God is concerned, the rich and the poor are all merged in the same pot, and God does not see you by what you have or do not have. God sees you for what you really are. Man looks on the outward appearance, but God looks upon the heart (1 Sam. 16:7). When you think of men like Howard Hughes who accumulated great wealth but died in loneliness, hurt, and despair, you realize that wealth is not what life is all about.

What is your philosophy? God is not against your having things, as long as things do not have you. If God can put things into your hands and allow you to be the steward or foreman who uses those things by orders from heaven, then He is not against trusting you with things. But most of us are not very trustworthy. He puts into our hands only what we are capable of managing. God is no respecter of persons. God loves all people alike.

● *Planning*—A third important feature to building credibility is planning. Verse 3 says, "A prudent man foreseeth the evil, and hideth himself." He has the ability to look down the road and see the consequences of his decisions and actions, and he hides himself. That is, he avoids unnecessary problems. "But the simple"—that is, those who are not availing themselves of the facts—"pass on" and pay the price. They rush ahead and are punished. We must plan if we are going to be successful. Success in life does not just happen. You plan it. You decide the principles and priorities that are important in your life. You get your relationships with God and men right. Then you learn how to work with your hands and do the necessary things. You learn where to go and where not to go, what to do, and what not to do. Then as you begin making decisions prayerfully, you look down the road to see what the consequences of today's decisions will be five years from now. The leader in any society is the person who sees farthest down the road. We have an obligation to plan.

● *Personality*—The fourth concept is personality. Verse 4 says, "By humility and the fear of the Lord are riches, and honor, and life." There are some people who must believe that God called them to persecute everybody else, and, verbally, that is all they ever do. They maliciously attack, gossip, slander, and libel. The whole of their life is one continuous hate campaign, and nobody can get along with them. No matter how you try, they are determined not to like you.

I have a friend whom I could not get to meet with some people. We were trying to heal a little situation. He said that he was afraid if he went to that meeting he would like them, and he did not want to do that! If people would just sit down and talk and pray, likely about 90 percent of our problems could be worked out. Personality, then, is very important in building personal relationships.

● *Parenting*—Another element that God says is a key to building credibility in our personal relationships is proper parenting. Verse 6 says, "Train up a child in the way he should go, and when he is old, he will not depart from it." How can a man be a successful preacher or businessman if he is not a successful daddy? A successful career woman must first be a successful mother, because that is first and foremost.

Verse 15 says that "foolishness is bound in the heart of a child, but the rod of correction shall drive it far from him." This refers to *rebellion.* Rebellion is bound in the heart of a little boy or little girl from the time he or she is born. How do you get that rebellion out? Well, Solomon said the rod of correction shall drive it far from him. Now I know that is not popular in today's world. We all abhor child abuse; there is nothing lower on this earth than an adult who will misuse and abuse a child. But there is one sure way of abusing your child, and that is by failing to correct him. We need to teach character and principles to our sons and daughters. If you love your children, you will correct them.

● *Business*—Next, let us consider building credibility in our business relationships. There are several principles mentioned in verse 7: "The rich ruleth over the poor, and the borrower is servant to the lender." Money cannot be your priority. If you are in business just to make money, the chances are you will fail. The Bible makes it clear that "the love of money is the root of all evil" (1 Tim. 6:10). If you are motivated only by making money, then your priorities are turned around. Your priority in business should not be the making of money, but that God might put things in your hands so you could be a blessing to others. Verse 9 says, "He that hath a bountiful eye shall be blessed, for he giveth of his bread to the poor." This is part of the philosophy of business relationships. Share what you have. Give to others and reach out to the poor. Do not let anybody in need pass you if it is in the power of your hand to help him, and God will honor you for that.

Then look at Proverbs 22:13: "The slothful man saith, There is a lion without; I shall be slain in the streets." The lazy man will not go out to work because of his fear that a lion will catch him and eat him alive. That was several thousand years ago. Today he makes excuses every bit as unreasonable. There are all kinds of excuses for not going to work. I believe we have an unemployment problem in America, but it is not as serious as you read about.

Notice verse 16: "He that oppresseth the poor to increase his riches, and he that giveth to the rich [or bribes the rich] shall surely come to want." Ill-gotten gain brings only regret.

● *Moral relationships*—Finally, we need to build credibility through our moral relationships. Verse 14 says, "The mouth of strange women is a deep pit." It is not easy today to take a stand for what is right, moral, and proper. God's basic standard of morality has not changed from the beginning.

Extramarital sex and premarital sex and homosexuality and promiscuous heterosexuality are just as wrong today as they were in the days these words were written in Proverbs. We do not have to change it one iota. If you want to build credibility, spend about sixty years together raising children and grandchildren and teaching them how to live, not just how to make a living. Set the example for them. Husbands, thank God for your wife, and, wives, thank God for your husband. Work together at creating and maintaining credibility in your moral relationships. If you do so, you will be seeing things from God's perspective.

How Not to Ruin Your Life

The most tragic thing about life is that it can be ruined and wasted. There is a motto that expresses the situation precisely: "Only one life, 'twill soon be past; only what's done for Christ will last." What a tragedy that so many waste their lives rather than live them for Christ and His cause. Unfortunately, many forces today are out to destroy your life. Solomon warns of these evils in chapter 23.

● *Beware of the world*—Verses 1-8 warn against being exploited by the world. How many lives have been wasted because they were exploited by a Christ-hating world! Solomon begins Proverbs 23 by warning of a ruler, or a wealthy person, who brings you into his home to bribe you. If he puts you at his table and puts all of the wonderful and dainty food before you, be careful. Do not fall for that. Do not let your stomach become your god. He has something in mind. He is trying to buy you and you should not be for sale. The lust of the flesh, the lust of the eyes, and the pride of life—according to 1 John 2:15-16—are the only three avenues by which Satan can approach you. But he is constantly doing that. That is how Satan fell, how Adam fell, and how everybody has fallen who has ever fallen.

I look at some who loved the Lord but who have sold out for money. Somehow they changed when they began to prosper materially. I see others who, because of the quest of a higher stratum of social life, sell out and are exploited by the world.

● *Watch associations*—Second, many lives are wasted and ruined by association with rebels. "Speak not in the ears of a fool [rebel], for he will despise the wisdom of thy words" (v. 9). How many do you know who, because of a bad association, have had their testimony influenced adversely or their ministry wrecked? I know many. In my counseling work, I am at times brought face to face with fine Christians who are spending a lot of time with a negative and rebellious believer. By so doing, these people hurt and damage only themselves.

Be careful of your associations, particularly if you are being impressed and influenced by unbelievers. That is why the Scripture says we are not to be "unequally yoked together with unbelievers" (2 Cor. 6:14). That has to do not only with marriage, but also applies to business relationships and to any other kind of relationship. Be careful—Scripture is clear. Association with rebels can waste and ruin your life.

● *Be honest*—And then, in verses 10 and 11, the subject of unprincipled business is addressed. "Remove not the old landmark." Do not move the boundary lines of uninformed, unintelligent, and unsophisticated people in order to take their properties away from them. Do not do people in financially and hurt those who are unable to defend themselves. Verse 11 reminds us that "their Redeemer is mighty; He shall plead their cause with thee." God is keeping a record book of all the poor and the unsophisticated who have been taken in by those who were talented in sleight-of-hand or who were dishonest in business. If you are in the kind of business where dishonesty is a requisite, get out of it. You would be far better off to be poor and honest than wealthy and dishonest.

● *Watch immoral relationships*—Verses 26-28 warn against immoral relationships. "My son, give me thine heart, and let thine eyes observe my ways. For a whore is a deep ditch; and a strange woman is a narrow pit. She also lieth in wait as for a prey, and increaseth the transgressors among men." In the ministry alone, scores of men once greatly used of God across this land and around the world, have traded their birthrights for messes of pottage, and in moments of pleasure they sold their testimony and their calling with it. What a tragedy!

But the rate of transgression is even greater in business. I see the business world out there with its professional massage parlors and the services of the prostitutes, and so on. Scripture says that of all the sins in which you can be involved, the one sin that will hurt you most and do you the most damage is the sin of immorality. All sins we commit, Paul tells us, are without or outside the body except immorality, and here we sin against the temple of God (1 Cor. 6:18-19).

When you are involved in immorality, you hurt the temple of God and the persons with whom you commit the sin. You cause scars that cannot be erased. Immoral relationships waste lives. Now, if you want to be successful in life and do not want to waste your life, be pure. Be biblical in your relationships. When you walk down that aisle with that one with whom you are going to live the rest of your life, let that be the first person you have ever known. If you have already gone beyond that ideal, then thank God for 1 John 1:7, "The blood of Jesus Christ, His Son, cleanseth us from all sin." Get a new beginning in Christ.

● *Shun drugs*—The final point in my division of chapter 23 (vv. 29-35) speaks of being victimized by drugs. We have a drugged society today, but since we are not honest enough to deal with it, we are not going to cure it nationally. Until we get honest about it, we are not going to get help. Now what do I mean that we are not honest about drugs? I suppose every right-thinking, intelligent person is against heroin. I am against heroin, hashish, pot, barbiturates, and all the other drugs that are wiping people out today. I am glad that young people are more conservative than their parents. According to a recent Gallup Poll, fewer young people than ever want decriminalization of marijuana usage. Marijuana is a drug. But we are not honest about the problem. Why? Because the number one drug in America, the one nobody talks about— including the legislators, the leaders, and most of all the preachers—is alcohol; and there are more people in the penitentiaries because of the abuse of alcohol than of any other drug. Tobacco was banned from advertising on television because it is bad for health. But we still have the booze and the beer advertised. They are still promoting drugs that not only destroy lungs and give cancer and all the illnesses that tobacco does, and they also promote that liquid drug that destroys minds, morals, and families, as well as bodies.

I admire the stand taken by professional golfer John Mahaffey, who won the Bob Hope Desert Classic in January 1984. As he approached the 1984 season, he determined to be a better player. He hadn't won since 1981. In addition to practicing with more determination, he made another important decision: no more drinking, smoking, and carousing. He quit the booze, stopped smoking—cold turkey—and at thirty-five years of age began to feel better than he did at twenty-five. He jokingly said he grew a mustache to have something to do with his hands. After winning the Bob Hope tournament, he had plenty to do with his hands: counting his $72,000 prize. I don't know anything about Mahaffey's relationship with God, but I congratulate him for seeing the light and quitting drinking and smoking. He is a better athlete and his mind is undoubtedly clearer. Would that the over-the-hill athletes who do the beer commercials were wiser!

Look at the description of the drinker in verse 29: "Who hath woe?" Who on earth is in more continual trouble than the fellow who drinks? "Who hath sorrow?" Who is always in deep trouble and has suffered great loss and is weeping? "Who hath contentions?" Who is always in an argument with somebody? "Who hath babbling?" Who is always running his mouth and saying nothing? "Who hath wounds without cause?" Who is always getting hurt physically unnecessarily? "Who hath redness of eyes? Those who tarry long at the wine," according to verse 30.

Those who hang around the taverns, the saloons, and the bars, and who store liquor at home, are the ones I call "bottle babies." They are the hooked generation. Be a part of the unhooked generation. You should be hooked on one thing only and that is Jesus Christ.

We are commanded not to look upon wine when it is fermented (v. 31). Do not look on it, touch it, or drink it by the thimbleful or the barrelful. You do not need it. Get up in the morning without a toddy to get going. Go to bed at night without going to the refrigerator. Live your day and make your decisions without leaning on anybody or anything but the Lord.

Verse 32 says alcoholic beverages bite "like a serpent." That means they poison you. They are deadly. I loved my daddy, and I stood by the bed as his hand dropped out of mine when he died of cirrhosis of the liver, the result of alcoholism. If you want to know what I think of alcohol, I hate it.

Solomon also notes that not only does it bite like a serpent and sting like an adder, it also causes you to be immoral. "Thine eyes shall behold strange women" (v. 33). This means any woman to whom you are not married. Alcohol makes your eyes seek after and lust after immorality. Your "heart shall utter perverse things." It puts vulgar words on your tongue. Some people act like two individuals. When they are sober, they are so gracious and sweet and kind and noble and considerate. But when they are drunk, they are just the opposite.

Verse 34 says, "Thou shalt be as he that lieth down in the midst of the sea." That is staggering. There is no stability, and you cannot hold on. Verse 35 says the drunkard will claim, "They have stricken me." They beat him, and he did not feel it.

But then when he wakes up, he says, "I will seek it yet again" (v. 35). There is nothing a man forgets any quicker than the terrible anguish he experienced during a drunken spree. So the next day he will do it again. The only cure for an alcoholic is the same as the cure for a homosexual, a liar, a thief, or anybody else who is a sinner—that includes all of us. The cure is the blood of Jesus Christ and the power of the indwelling Holy Spirit. Without that there is no hope of rescuing one from a ruined life. May God deliver us from the things that will ruin and wreck our lives.

God's Perspective on Man's World

The Bible tells us not only how to live as individuals but also how to live as nations, how to relate to one another internationally, how to succeed in our families, and how to succeed in our communities. If every leader in every area of government—local, state, and national—would get acquainted with the Bible, we could have successful countries, governments, homes, and business enterprises. We could live in peace and all the needs of the poor could be provided, and we would never have war. I am speaking of the ideal, but there is coming a day when all of that will be so. One day we will have a perfect government. There is coming a day when we will have perfect economy, perfect health, and no war because men will beat their weapons of war into instruments of peace. That day is coming when Jesus Christ, the Prince of Peace, sits down upon the throne of David in Jerusalem and the saints of God rule and reign with Him for a thousand years. After that comes eternity.

That is the future, but I am also interested in the here and now. Proverbs 24 has plenty to say on that subject. There are three key verses in Proverbs 24.

● *Don't faint*—The first one is Proverbs 24:10: "If thou faint in the day of adversity, thy strength is small." I have often said that a man's greatness is not determined by his talent or by his wealth, but rather by what it takes to discourage him. Everybody has trouble. Harry Truman used to say, "If you can't stand the grease, get out of the kitchen." Every child of God needs to learn how to stand the grease. Jack Hyles, a Chicago area pastor, often says, "There are two words that ought not be in the Christian's vocabulary, and those two words are *quit* and *can't*."

● *Don't strike out*—The second key verse: "For a just man falleth seven times, and riseth up again: but the wicked shall fall into mischief" (v. 16). The child of God has the promise that, though he may have two strikes against him, he need not strike out. God always causes us to triumph (2 Cor. 2:14), and it is often darkest just before the dawn. Hang on a little longer and trust God. He will give the victory.

● *Respect God and government*—Key verse three: "My son, fear thou the Lord and the king, and meddle not with them that are given to change" (v. 21). We are to respect and honor God and respect and honor civil government, and we are warned not to associate with radicals. Every young person needs to heed that. We have an obligation to be good Christians, to obey the Lord, to be good citizens, and to obey government unless government requires that we disobey the

Law of God. Then we revert to the higher authority.

Wisdom, Understanding, and Knowledge

Chapter 24 itself may be divided into three parts by its subject matter. In verses 3-4, Solomon says, "Through *wisdom* is an house builded, and by *understanding* it is established, and by *knowledge* shall the chambers be filled with all precious and pleasant riches."

● The first point is to see business from God's perspective. Being a Christian businessman or woman can be as important a calling as the ministry of the Gospel. And if God wants you there, He wants you to be successful. I believe in capitalism and the free enterprise system and private property ownership. I do not believe that the state should own people. I do believe that people should have the right to own property, to work hard, to achieve, to earn, and to win. These are some of the initiatives that are built into what we know as the free-enterprise system.

There are several other verses regarding the business perspective. "Prepare thy work without, and make it fit for thyself in the field; and afterwards build thine house" (v. 27). How important that is. A young man runs off into business and before his business shows a profit, he buys a brand new $20,000 car and $100,000 house. Then he cannot make his personal payments, and so his business goes down. God's perspective on business is very clear. Develop your business first. Build your home and buy your car last. Drive an old clunker around. Live in a small apartment. The first several years of our married life, my wife and I lived in a two-room apartment as I was working to get the church started. The business of the Lord's work was more important than how well we lived.

Verses 30-34 tell quite a story. "I went by the field of the slothful, and by the vineyard of the man void of understanding" (v. 30). Weeds had taken over, and nothing was happening; there was no production. Verse 32 says, "I saw," or "I came to a conclusion," and the conclusion is in verses 33-34: "A little sleep, a little slumber, a little folding of the hands to sleep: so shall thy poverty come as one that travelleth; and thy want as an armed man."

Poverty will break in on you like an armed robber—so suddenly you will wonder how it ever happened. You should not expect something given to you. We have a crowd in this country who would not work in a bakery eating the holes out of doughtnuts.

As Evangelist B.R. Lakin said, "God's plan for the poverty program is work." And he would have known after more than sixty years in the ministry.

• Next, let us go back to see God's perspective for the military. Verses 5-6 say, "A wise man is strong; yea, a man of knowledge increaseth strength. For by wise counsel thou shalt make thy war, and in multitude of counselors there is safety." Is war ever in the will of God? Now I hope we never get into another war, but whenever the freedoms and the liberties of a God-fearing nation are in danger, war is in the will of God. There is something worse than war, and that is slavery. I would rather be dead than Red, and I think that we have a biblical mandate to protect our children. Scripture says if a man will not provide or care for or protect his children and his family, he is worse than an infidel (1 Tim. 5:8). I believe in military preparedness while working for peace. That is where the multitude of counselors comes in. But at the same time we need the wisdom to be strong in order to guarantee that our children and grandchildren grow up in a free society.

• Finally, the third point is God's perspective on social issues. Verses 11-12 say, "If thou forbear to deliever them that are drawn unto death, and those that are already to be slain; if thou sayest, Behold, we knew it not; doth not He that pondereth the heart consider it? And He that keepeth thy soul, doth not He know it? And shall not He render to every man according to his works?" Do we have an obligation to the poor? We absolutely do, not only in America, but in every part of the world. That is why the church I pastor is involved in sixty-five nations, often working with refugees. We go to the poor. In our own nation we work in the inner cities to aid both the temporal and spiritual needs of people. The goal of the Gospel is world evangelization.

I am often asked why I am always addressing the issues of abortion. As pointed out, 1.5 million babies die every year in this country *legally!* Nearly 15 million have died since the 1973 court ruling legalizing murder-on-demand. Why am I battling that? Because of verse 11. "If thou forbear to deliver them that are drawn unto death." If you keep your mouth shut, saying it is not your business, God will render to you according to your works (v. 12). God will judge me, Jerry Falwell, if I keep my mouth shut. It would be far more palatable and popular for me to keep quiet on things like abortion, prayer in schools, pornography, and illegal drugs; but if I did, God Almighty would judge me. I have an obligation to preach the Gospel to every creature and to lift up the biblical standard of righteousness so there is a standard of morality in our society. Christians are the salt of the earth. We are supposed to produce thirst and kill weeds in the process. We have an obligation to help the helpless.

If we go God's way by following the Scriptures, we can, from God's perspective, have a healthy society. Living by God's principles promotes a nation to greatness. Violating God's principles brings a nation to shame. May God give us the courage to stand for those things that will promote our nation onto the path that is in God's perspective.

10

How to Deal with People
Proverbs 25—27

We live in a world of 4.7 billion people. The only successful people on this planet are those who have learned to love and to relate to people. Every relationship on this earth that is important has to do with people. Of course, we have our vertical relationship with God, but we also have horizontal relationships. Every successful person in the world, in any field, is a person who knows how to relate to and to interact with other people.

I love people. I am glad God called me to be a pastor. I speak to millions of people every week through the media, and I speak to many thousands of people every week in person. I enjoy meeting people. I am usually the last person to leave a meeting, because God has given me a love for people. I would submit to you that in your work, whatever it is, if you do not love being around people, communicating with people, and relating to people, you are a failure. I know many pastors who can stay in one place only a short time—two or three years at the most—because they have not learned to love and get along with people. They wear out their welcome, and it is good-bye and off they go, supposedly led by the Lord to another ministry. Though God may direct some pastors to move on, I think it is great to have a love affair with people and to be able to stay in the same place for life. You still have the same friends you had when you started and add a lot of new ones along the way. There are 21,000 members in the church I pastor. Although I cannot greet each person by name, I can honestly say that I love every one.

Being a Good Leader

Proverbs 25:5 tells us that leaders need to get along with people: "Take away the wicked from before the king, and his throne shall be established in righteousness." That suggests getting all the crooked cronies away from the President, the king, congressmen, governors, and other leaders. Do not let them be insulated from the populace by dishonest people.

● *Good communications*—A good leader has good communications with those he leads. He knows when they are hurting, and he cares. He is aware of the people and what they are thinking. No one can be a good pastor until he develops a spiritual perception of what is happening in the congregation. Are they happy? Are they sad? Is there discontent? Is there a particular need among the people? Are they discouraged? He has to be spiritually able to feel what they feel. For that reason a good pastor will depend on capable people to be sounding boards of what is going on in the congregation.

Leaders need to know they can be wrong, and they need to be in touch with the people so that the leaders can hear when they are wrong and do something about it. That is what Solomon is saying here: "Take away the wicked from before the king." We are told in 1 Timothy 2 to pray for the President, the king, the one in authority, and for all those in government. We should pray that God will give them wisdom, protect them, and speak to them. We also need to pray that God will give wisdom to the leaders to associate themselves with the right kinds of people. A good leader can have bad people around him and fail, not because his heart was not right or because he had bad motives, but because those around him would not allow any communication to come through to him that they did not agree with or believe in.

I thank God for the four or five people who work closely with me, almost on a daily basis. They are not afraid to tell me exactly what I need to hear, not what I want to hear. And for that reason I am able to stay in touch with the people I pastor.

● *Good relations*—Second, Solomon speaks of getting along with your neighbors in verses 8-10: "Go not forth hastily to strive." Do not run to court quickly to sue your brother, "lest thou know not what to do in the end thereof, when thy neighbor hath put thee to shame. Debate thy cause with thy neighbor himself." Go to him privately and do not talk to everybody about the problem between the two of you, "lest he that heareth it put thee to shame, and thine infamy turn not away." These verses concern getting along with your neighbors. You say I do not have many neighbors. Geographically, of course, Solomon is talking about the houses next to you, across the street, and behind you. But he is also talking about those neighbors with whom you work, or attend school, or play, or spend leisure time, or whatever. He is talking about the people with whom you come in contact every day.

What are the principles involved? First, when your neighbor wrongs you, whether verbally or in action, do not run to the outside world, to a courtroom, or to the public. Go to the person, and go quietly. Do not discuss it with other friends, where you try to debate the cause and correct the problem.

There is a great deal going on today in the area of lawsuits between believers. Now the Scriptures are very clear about that (1 Cor. 6:1-8). If my brother wrongs me and even costs me some money, I have no right to take him to court. That is what Paul says. Do not take your brother to law. It is far better to lose the money than to violate the Scripture and lose your testimony.

When you follow the scriptural plan, God makes it up to you. You may lose a thousand dollars here, but God will make it up with two thousand over yonder because you did the right thing. Christians need to realize that the Bible has the prescription to correct problems between brethren: Go to your brother, confess your fault, and try to bring about a reconciliation. If he will not hear you, that is his problem, but you have cleared your conscience with God. If he has wronged you financially and will not be honest about it, pray for him. Ask God to speak to him, but do not take him to court. God will take him to court one day.

● *Dealing with yourself*—Point three is about how to deal with yourself. I do not have as much of a problem with politicians and neighbors as I do with the fellow I shave every morning. That is probably about the way it is with all of us. There is a war going on constantly within us between the flesh and the Spirit. The Spirit wants us to do what is right. The flesh wants to do what is wrong. Each day as we feed on the Word of God and pray, we can look to God for the victory. Christ is Lord, and we can overrule the flesh in the power of His name.

Notice verse 16: "Hast thou found honey? Eat so much as is sufficient for thee, lest thou be filled therewith, and vomit it." When people start saying nice things about you and pouring that sweet wonderful praise on you, do not swallow too much of it. It will make you and those around you nauseous.

Another problem we have with ourselves is expressed in verse 28: "He that hath no rule over his own spirit is like a city that is broken down, and without walls." This is a lack of self-control. To have no control over the flesh, over your habits, your attitudes and actions, the places you go, and the things you do is a shame. Verses 16 and 28 warn us to watch out for our egos. I think I have the best wife and three children in the whole world, but if you agree with that, there is something wrong with you. We should each consider our own families to be the best. That is not egotistical, but rather just the common love that should exist in a home. Yet, we must not paint a nonexistent picture of their greatness, talents, and abilities. That can create an unreasonable struggle to achieve an unrealistic goal.

● *Dealing with enemies*—Finally, let us examine verses 21-22, relating to dealing with your enemies. Do you have anybody who does not like you? If you do, here is how to deal with it. Solomon says, "If thine enemy be hungry, give him bread to eat; and if he be thirsty, give him water to drink, for thou shalt heap coals of fire upon his head, and the Lord shall reward thee." How do you deal with enemies? Do you rejoice when they fall? I can honestly say that when I hear from time to time that some critic of mine is experiencing misfortune, I feel remorse, not joy.

We all have critics, and it is especially difficult for them to understand how we can be against sin while loving sinners. They do not understand how you can hate alcoholism and drunkenness but love drunkards, or that you can hate homosexuality and still love homosexuals. I had a debate once on "Donahue" on that very subject, and someone in the audience said you cannot love somebody and hate what they do. This is conditional love. I asked her the question, "Do you love thieves?"

"Of course, I do," was her reply.

"Do you love stealing?"

"Of course not."

All I am saying is you can hate sin and love sinners. We

cannot have contempt for anybody. We cannot be bitter or hateful toward anybody, no matter what he or she is doing. At the same time, we cannot lower the flag for the sake of "togetherness" and forget that there is a biblical standard of right and wrong.

Four Bad Characters

There are four bad characters spoken of in Proverbs 26. Even though they were prevalent in Solomon's day, they still exist in our own time. They are (1) the rebel (vv. 1-11); (2) the egotist (v. 12); (3) the bum (vv. 13-16); and (4) the busybody (vv. 17-28).

● *The rebel*—The first bad fellow mentioned in the chapter is the fool, or, perhaps better translated, the rebel, in verses 1-11. Why does Solomon spend so much time talking about the rebel? The answer is that God just cannot use rebellious people. In our society today, we have young people who rebel against their parents. Others rebel against civil government. We also have a group who rebel against the leadership of pastors and teachers. Solomon, under divine inspiration, tells us throughout the Book of Proverbs that a rebellious spirit is a bad thing.

God has placed us under parents, teachers, government, and spiritual leaders. Those persons represent the institutions of the home, school, civil government, and church. There will never be a time when God does not have somebody over you. I answer to those who are over me. Even the President of the United States answers to the laws of the land, the Constitution, the Congress, the Supreme Court, and the people. Of course, he answers to God as we all do. We are all supposed to be in subjection to authority, and whenever we refuse to submit to that God-appointed authority, we become dishonorable.

Why are there so many drug addicts today? Why is there a

herpes epidemic now infesting some 20 million Americans? The rebellion of the '60s and '70s has brought the judgment of God upon this nation in the '80s. Rebellion always does that.

Then verse 3 speaks of "a whip for the horse, a bridle for the ass, and a rod for the fool's back." The rebel is undisciplined. He does not want any rules and regulations. He is not going to be subjected to what he calls "legalism." Nobody is going to tell him what to do, and so he becomes an undisciplined person. He often finds himself victimzied by booze or by drugs, or he finds his lungs filled with cancer because of tobacco and nicotine. He finds his mind wiped out because his hedonism and addiction to drugs has destroyed the marvelous thing that God has given him—his brain. He allows himself, because of his undisciplined ways, to become at odds with everybody so that nobody likes him. He then becomes depressed and isolated.

Verse 6 says, "He that sendeth a message by the hand of a fool cutteth off the feet, and drinketh damage." In other words, to send a message to someone by way of a rebel is like cutting off your own feet or drinking poison. A rebel is an unreliable person. You cannot depend on a cantankerous, rebellious person. He is not going to be faithful and loyal. You never know when he is going to have the next explosion— mentally or emotionally.

Then verse 11 reads, "As a dog returneth to his vomit, so a fool returneth to his folly." A hardheaded, rebellious person is unteachable. One of the greatest traits of a leader is that he is always teachable. He must always be open to further insight and instruction—he must never feel that he knows more than everybody else.

● *The egotist*—Second, we meet the egotist. Even though Solomon had a lot of bad things to say about the rebel, the egotist is worse. "Seest thou a man who is wise in his own conceit? There is more hope of a fool than of him" (v. 12). A conceited, egotistical person knows everything, has all the answers, cares only about himself, and is always promoting his own thing.

I have learned as a pastor that team effort is necessary to succeed in pastoring a church, leading a school, or heading up an international ministry. One thing I admire in the leadership of our ministry in Lynchburg is the team spirit. There is a unity of purpose to serve the Lord Jesus Christ rather than ourselves. We must either work together as a team or we do not function properly at all.

The same is true in a family. There is no big shot in the family. Mom, Dad, and the children are all equally important, and having your own way is not so important. What is important is that the family is promoted and provided for and that God honors that family. May God deliver us from thinking too highly of ourselves and from thinking that we know more than others.

Talking to a pastor who needed somebody to fill a large position in the Lord's work, I made a recommendation. "What about Pastor So-and-so."

He replied, "The guy is such a puffed-up egotist that our people cannot even stand to hear him. He gets up and tells about what he is doing, where he is going, how much he has, what he knows, and brag, brag, brag!"

There is nothing more obnoxious than a braggadocious spirit.

● *The bum*—We have observed two bad characters in Proverbs 26—the rebel and the egotist. We now come to the bum in verses 13-16. We could call him by a nicer term, but in reality he is just a bum. Verse 13 says, "The slothful man saith, There is a lion in the way." He says, "I cannot go to work today. I will get hurt. A lion may get me. It is too dangerous."

First of all, the bum is full of excuses. It is true that we have a bad unemployment problem in this country. There are some sincere people who would like to be working who simply cannot find work, though they are earnestly looking for it. However, if all the people who really do not want to work but just want to draw a paycheck were cut from unemployment figures, the real unemployment rate might be cut in half.

I think we have raised up a generation of bums full of excuses. We ought to help the aged and the sick. We ought to have welfare for those who need help and are truly deserving. I am not against the Social Security system. We ought to help those who are looking for work and cannot find it, but there is a segment out there that is draining and sapping the blood out of a free-enterprise society, and I call them bums.

Solomon says something else about the bum in verse 14: "As the door turneth upon his hinges, so doth the slothful upon his bed." The bum is as locked and latched to his bed as the door is to its hinges. If the phone rings, he is going to have that phone right by the bed so he does not have to put his feet on the floor and possibly catch a cold. If there is something to eat, he will have a little tray there so he can sit and eat on the side of the bed. If you call him at 8 A.M. or 10 A.M. or 1 P.M., likely he will be in that bed. Not only is he full of excuses, but he is bedfast.

There is something else about this bum in verse 15: "The slothful hideth his hand in his bosom; it grieveth him to bring it again to his mouth." I said the rebel was a bad guy. Solomon said the egotist was worse, but we have gotten down to the bum now. We are heading right for the cellar. This fellow is lazy. There are very few hopeless people in this world, but a lazy man is apt to be one of them. I do not mean to imply that a lazy person cannot get over it. I just have not met many who have I believe a lazy person can get motivation from the

Holy Spirit to get up and go again, but not many of them ever do.

Verse 16 adds that "the sluggard is wiser in his own conceit than seven men that can render a reason." He knows more than anybody else. He, like the rebel, is unteachable. It is hard to teach a bum anything. You can preach, teach, shout, and set the example, and the lazy person can lie down beside work all day and never be bothered by it. May God deliver us from being bums.

● *The busybody*—Finally, we come to the fourth bad fellow in Proverbs 26. Beginning with verse 17, he is identified as the busybody. "He that passeth by, and meddleth with strife belonging not to him, is like one that taketh a dog by the ears." The fellow who is always minding somebody else's business will get bitten or hurt, because it is like picking a dog up by the ears. The fellow who is always meddling with somebody else's business is in trouble constantly.

Verse 19 mentions something else: "So is the man that deceiveth his neighbor, and saith, Am not I in sport?" Verse 18 says he is always casting "firebrands, arrows, and death." He is guilty of gossip, but when he gets caught telling one of his tales he says, "Am not I in sport? I was just kidding. I did not really mean it." He is always spreading poison. Do you know a man or a woman like that who is always gossiping?

You know, in some churches today the pastor would be well within his rights to deliver a pastoral edict that all members have their telephones removed for thirty days. This would allow some of the gossips to get through their withdrawals and learn what to do with the six hours a day they have been using on the telephone. They could get reoriented in a sort of sobering-up period for a busybody. We always have an idea that this is a job for ladies. Men are just as guilty of this as women. There is no difference, because it is part of fallen human nature. May God deliver us from it.

Then, verse 23 notes that "burning lips and a wicked heart are like potsherd covered with silver dross." A busybody has a hard time recognizing the truth. He can get so accustomed to telling wild tales that he believes them himself. He can get into a fantasy world where he does not recognize the truth coming down the highway.

But there is something else about the busybody: "He that hateth dissembleth with his lips, and layeth up deceit within him" (v. 24). The person who is a busybody is full of hate and deceit. When he is talking very kindly and graciously, do not believe him, because there are abominations in his heart.

What is Solomon telling us about these people? He is saying that if that happens to be you—and it is very possible that born-again people can have these afflictions—determine under God that this is not going to afflict you anymore. Determine that with God's help you will be delivered from this negativism. Decide with God's help that you will not be a rebel, or an egotist, or a bum, or a busybody. May God help us to be the right kind of person for Him.

Winning Friends and Influencing People

Who does not want to have friends? I certainly have never had any desire to be a hermit or hide away in a cave. God did not call me to isolation. We should constantly be finding and making friends and influencing people for good. Solomon approaches the subject by telling us how not to win friends.

● *Don't brag*—If you are going to win friends and influence people, do not be a braggart. Stop telling everybody how great you are, by raising up your own flag and promoting yourself. First, do not boast about the future. "Boast not thyself of tomorrow, for thou knowest not what a day may bring forth" (27:1). When I tell somebody I will see them tomorrow, I automatically add, "The Lord willing." Even if you do not say that it ought certainly to be in your heart and thoughts. That is the only guarantee any of us has to do anything one moment from right now. The moment I have is this moment. We are all just one heartbeat from eternity. When you hear someone bragging about what he is going to do tomorrow and the next day and the next month, he does not understand who he is or who God is.

Verse 2 says, "Let another man praise thee." Do not praise yourself. Let a stranger or someone else do it. Not only should we not boast about tomorrow, we should not boast about our talents and abilities. We do not have anything but what God has given us. You are nothing more than God Almighty enables you to be. God gave you those talents, those hands, that mind—and just as quickly, God can take it all away.

Nationally, we are somewhat proud and cocky. Our liberties are a gift of God and could be taken from us in an instant. You could have been born in Russia or Cuba or China, but God allowed you to be freeborn. Do not boast or brag about anything. Everything that God has put into our hands is from Him, and we ought to use it to help others. I think we have an obligation to the world that is under the hammer and the sickle to lift up a standard of hope for them. Everything we have came from God.

● *Shun evil*—Second, if we are to win friends and influence people, we must not envy others. Jealousy is even worse than anger, according to verses 3-4: "A stone is heavy, and the sand weighty; but a fool's wrath is heavier than them both. Wrath is cruel, and anger is outrageous; but who is able to stand before envy?" I have some pastor friends who just cannot have a good associate pastor because they are jealous of any attention that goes to the associate. It works in the family that way too. There are mothers who are jealous of the attention their husbands give to the children, and there are husbands who are jealous of the attention mothers give to the children.

Some are jealous because other members of the family are prospering. There are neighbors jealous of another because he has a better automobile or a better house. It is true in the business world, and, sad to say, it is true in the family of God.

● *Promote people*—The way to really help people to like you is to promote them. Do not be the top, but be the least. Let others do most of the talking—you do most of the listening. And when you hear they are succeeding in something, do not feel bad about it, but thank God for it. Pick up the phone and congratulate them.

Other Pointers
The third part of Proverbs 27 deals with one's background and upbringing.

● *Don't forsake your roots*—Verse 5-10 tell us not to forsake our roots; we should not be ashamed of a humble upbringing.

My mother was one of sixteen children. They were reared in a farmhouse in Appomattox County in a little place called Hollywood, Virginia. It is not much like the other Hollywood. When everybody was home, about 300 people were there. Kids walked to school three or four miles a day, through snow and all other kinds of weather, to a one-room schoolhouse. Mother went only as far as the fifth grade because she, like all the others, had to work to keep food on the table. My father made it to the sixth grade. But I am thankful for my father and mother and grandparents. Never lose sight of where you came from. Then you might be able to appreciate a little more what God has done for you. Do not be like the "bird that wandereth from her nest" or like the "man that wandereth from his place" (v. 8). Remember, and be thankful for your roots.

Verse 10 adds another note: "Thine own friend, and thy father's friend, forsake not." When an elderly person walks up to me somewhere and says, "I was a friend of your daddy," he does not have to say anymore. He is my friend right away.

So, if you want to have friends, Solomon says, "Do not brag, do not envy, do not forsake your roots."

● *Don't nag*—Solomon was an expert in this when it came to women; he had 300 wives. He wrote that "a continual dropping in a very rainy day and a contentious woman are alike. Whosoever hideth her hideth the wind, and the ointment of his right hand, which betrayeth itself" (vv. 15-16). A nagging woman and a continual dropping on a rainy day are much alike, and to try to quiet her is like trying to hold the wind or to hold onto a pig when your hands are greasy. When you have ointment on your hand, it is nearly impossible to hold something. Trying to contain the wind is just as unreasonable as trying to stop a nagging woman.

Now I want to reverse that, because perhaps Solomon was in a bad mood when he wrote this. Nagging men are the same way. There is nothing that will cause people to dislike you anymore than to be a nagging person. Nagging never helps people along. Encouragement, instruction, and example are far more productive than nagging. If you are going to win friends and influence people, replace nagging with love and prayer. By the way, nagging is not just a home phenomenon. A church is the same way, and so is a business enterprise. Nagging will not produce the results you seek. People have to see love, character, integrity, and leadership in *you.* You have to set the example for others.

● *Shun wrong friends*—Solomon goes on in verse 19 to warn against running with the wrong crowd: "As in water [like a mirror] face answereth to face, so the heart of man to man." Just as we see ourselves reflected in a still pool, we need to associate with people whose hearts and attitudes and spirits reflect our own. That is just another way of saying that "birds of a feather flock together." Bad associations can hurt and ruin you. You will not win others by capitulating to their weaknesses or by emulating their faults; they must respect you because you do not do what they do. Be careful of following the wrong crowd.

● *Avoid being too ambitious*—In verses 20-21, Solomon warns about unbridled ambition. Do not be too ambitious. "Hell and destruction are never full; so the eyes of man [the ambition of an uncontrolled, undisciplined person] are never satisfied. As the fining pot for silver, and the furnace for gold, so is the man to his praise." You can tell what kind of a person one is by the way he responds to praise of himself. Does he believe his own press reports? Does he think he is as great as his friends come up and tell him he is? How does he respond to praise when he does something outstanding? Is his response cocky and arrogant when people praise him, or does he realize that tomorrow there may be other difficulties that will bring him down off that perch? Just as the fining pot purifies silver and the furnace purifies gold, praise should purify a man, not promote him to arrogance. Just as hell and destruction are never full, the man who is ambitious and who wants to be number one in everything for his own sake will find that his ambitions and undisciplined ways will ruin and wreck him.

Another thing to remember: Do not let your ambitions outweigh your principles. You need never do the right thing in the wrong way. The end does not justify the means. You can alway do the right thing in the right way to accomplish the right and desired end. You do not have to take shortcuts. You do not have to violate your principles. You can win without ever compromising your views and values.

A businessman told me that he could not live the Christian life in business. There were shady deals and social drinking and all the rest. I told him that he needed the character to lovingly take a stand, but not in self-righteousness. I believe he would be respected for his stand and would not lose a thing. But if, on the other hand, demands were made with which a Christian could not comply, then he should quit the job and trust God to give him gainful employment in another opportunity in which he could honor the Lord. You do not ever have to do wrong.

● *Don't be careless*—Finally, in verses 23 to 27, Solomon warns, "Do not be careless." He goes on to say, "Be thou diligent to know the state of thy flocks, and look well to thy herds. For riches are not forever, and doth the crown endure to every generation?" In other words, do not be careless with what God has put in your hands. You have an obligation to your family to care for them, even in a time of unemployment. If I were out of work and could not find work commensurate with my training and abilities, I would look for something apart from my training and abilities, like digging ditches, or washing cars, or cutting lawns, or whatever it takes. I would much prefer to earn money to take care of my family by blistering my hands than to take a handout from anybody. If you are going to succeed as a person, you cannot afford to be careless.

Do you know why the boss succeeds? He is usually the guy who gets there first, leaves last, and does all the sweating. When you go home on Friday, he spends the weekend trying to figure ways to make the next payroll. He is the one who is on the phone day and night to keep the doors open. The successful boss is the one who does not have a position, but he has a calling. He has an area of responsibility. He is a hard, diligent worker. Do not be careless. Whatever God puts into your hands, use it for His glory.

If we would win friends and influence people properly, we should learn to heed Solomon's wise admonitions in Proverbs 27. We will be better servants of the Master when we abide by His rules. May He give us the grace to do so.

11

Good Leaders and Good Listeners

Proverbs 28—29

Everything rises and falls on leadership. In our families, homes, churches, schools, and in our nation today we need good leadership. Solomon gives us a number of necessary principles for good leaderhip in Proverbs 28.

Verse 15 is a key verse. "As a roaring lion, and a ranging bear; so is a wicked ruler over the poor people." Today we have the Castros, the Chernenkos, the Khadafys, and the Arafats who have little respect for human life. But there is a King of kings and Lord of lords in heaven who is keeping the books. One day Castro, Chernenko, Khadafy, and Arafat, will bow and confess that Jesus Christ is Lord, to the glory of God the Father (Rom. 14:11; Phil. 2:11).

But until that day, every one of us is a leader in some capacity. As a father and a husband, I have an obligation to be a leader in my home. Every parent has an obligation to be a spiritual leader in the home. But beyond that, all political leaders in this land and around the world are the ministers of God, whether they know it or not (Rom. 13:1). As a result, they are responsible to God and will one day answer to Him for the way they administer that leadership position.

Solomon gives us a number of principles of good leadership. First of all, a good leader must be stable. "The wicked flee when no man pursueth" (v. 1). Did you ever see a fellow always looking over his shoulder? That comes from a guilty conscience, from knowing something he hopes others are not aware of. That comes from what he has done in the past and has covered up. The wicked man, the one who violates the Law of God, is running when nobody is chasing him. He is defensive and always covering up. A good leader must be stable.

Verse 2 says, "For the transgression of a land many are the princes thereof: but by a man of understanding and knowledge the state thereof shall be prolonged." That simply means that when the Law of God is broken or transgressed, there are many administrations. They come and go. "Many are the princes thereof." South America, Italy, and a few other places have had scores of governments just since World War II. It makes you wonder if perhaps verse 2 applies there. In areas where the Khadafy-type persons are in leadership, very few ever go out of office by democratic process or by dying of old age. One leader simply follows another, breaking the Law of God. They are violating all the principles of leadership, and the administration is unstable.

I believe if we are going to have stability in this nation, we must have stable leadersip in our families, churches, and educational institutions. We need leaders who are stable. Notice the last part of verse 2: "But by a man of understanding and knowledge the state thereof shall be prolonged." There is stability when the leadership knows what it believes and stands on truth and the principles of righteousness.

A good leader also must have compassion. Verse 3 says, "A poor man that oppresseth the poor is like a sweeping rain which leaveth no food." When I think of a poor man getting in power, I think of Mr. Castro down in Cuba. He was supposed to replace Batista and be the savior and deliverer of the Cuban people. The American press was talking about that great liberator, Fidel Castro. Some intelligent people said no, that he was a Marxist. But they were shouted down by the American media. We soon found out that he was just a ditto of Khrushchev.

When a poor man who comes out of nothing, rises to power, and becomes all-powerful and oppresses the poor, he is like a sweeping rain that leaves nothing behind. Now the people of Cuba are in horrible condition, far worse than they were. And that does not condone the former dictatorship. The same was true of the Shah of Iran. I did not like all the things he did over there, and I did not approve of the way he ran the country, but I would take ten Shahs to one Khomeini, as any sensible person would. And yet the American press that berated the Shah of Iran was strangely silent about the vicious theocratic monster, the Ayatollah Khomeini. They got what they wanted.

Verse 8 speaks of being equitable: "He that by usury and unjust gain increaseth his substance [he who exploits the poor and the helpless], he shall gather it for him that will pity the poor." The man who goes out and robs the poor and takes away from the helpless will have that spoil taken from him by God Almighty, who will give it to somebody who will use it for the poor. God is the Advocate of the poor; He pleads their case. We need to be equitable if we are going to be leaders. We must be fair in our families as well as in our churches and our businesses. If God has made you an employer, be fair. On the other hand, if you are in labor, be fair. The day of something for nothing is over. Everyone is going to have to produce if this country is going to make it. Labor and management must both be equitable.

Then, a good leader must be honest. Verse 13 says, "He

that covereth his sins shall not prosper: but whoso confesseth and forsaketh them shall have mercy." God knows that in government today we need honesty. I am amazed at how we constantly talk about more treaties with the Soviet Union. The Russians have broken every treaty we have made with them.

And we must ask God to give us honorable leaders if we are to bring ourselves back to the place where God can one more time bless us and our families and churches and nation.

Another principle of leadership is found in verse 19: "He that tilleth his land shall have plenty of bread: but he that followeth after vain persons [runs with the wrong crowd] shall have poverty enough." Good leaders must be diligent. A successful businessman comes in earlier and leaves later than the rest of the crowd. He carries the burdens of his employees and seeks to make the payroll for their welfare. A good father is one who has decided to be responsible for others, not a responsibility to others. He assumes the obligations of feeding, caring for, and protecting his wife and children.

Leadership is earned, not taken. People will respect you when you earn that right to be respected as a leader. Diligent, hard workers become leaders and, unless you are a diligent, hard worker who is willing to put hours into what you are doing, you are not going to make it. I am fifty years old. If I look older, it is because I have a lot more mileage on me than that! I believe that is what Scripture is teaching here. To be a leader, you must be a worker. People have got to believe a man deserves to be followed, not just for a week or a month, but for his whole life. I am often asked about why I do not have a retirement plan. I do not plan to retire. I am just going to stay at it and keep on keeping on until I burn out or get blown out. A leader needs to be diligent.

Finally, a leader must be family-centered. In order to be a true leader, one must understand that the family is God's

basic unit in a civilized society. Under God, the family must
be the leader's number-one priority. Verse 24 says, "Whoso
robbeth his father or his mother, and saith, It is no transgression; the same is the companion of a destroyer."

Your mom and dad will be old one day, just as you will be,
and it would be very easy to take advantage of them. When
they get a little sick, you could just shove them out somewhere. I certainly believe that there is a place for nursing
homes, but there are a lot of times when taking Mom or Dad
into the house with you would be better.

A leader must be family centered. He must have his
interest in the family. He must love his wife and love his
children. A wife must love her husband, love her children.
When I go into a home, it does not take a great deal of time to
determine if there is love there—if they all really love each
other. If you cannot cut it at home, you cannot cut it in
leadership. If a man does not love his wife or his children and
does not treat them right, why do you think he will treat
anybody else right? A good leader first demonstrates leadership at home by love, concern, interest, and communication.
These big-time businessmen and politicians and actors and
actresses who are not giving five minutes of time to their
family and children have, sad to say, disqualified themselves
as leaders.

If we want to be leaders—and all of us are leaders in one
way or another—then let us practice the principles of good
leadership. A good leader is stable, exercises compassion for
others, is fair toward all, is honest in all his dealings, is a
diligent worker, and makes his family a top priority under the
Lord. How do you measure up to those qualities of leadership? You cannot measure up at all if you are not yet a
Christian. If you are a Christian, then ask God to help you be
the leader you know He wants you to be in every area of your
life.

How to Be a Good Listener

The fact that God gave man two ears and only one mouth may be an indication that He intended for us to do more listening than talking. In Proverbs 29 Solomon gives us some advice about becoming good listeners. The very first verse is a warning of what will happen when we fail to listen: "He, that being often reproved hardeneth his neck, shall suddenly be destroyed, and that without remedy." The man or woman who had been warned and rebuked often but disregards all advise and counsel will finally self-destruct.

Consider the necessity of listening to family authority. Verse 3 says, "Whoso loveth wisdom rejoiceth his father: but he that keepeth company with harlots spendeth his substance." Not only are we as Christians told by Solomon under divine inspiration to obey civil authority, but we are to listen to family authority. What is the family authority? Although this is absolutely devastating to the feminists of our day, and it is hard to say it in a way that the feminists do not twist it, I must declare what the Bible teaches. Yes, God has appointed the husband and father to be head of the home.

God never called the husband in the family to be a dictator. God has never called the husband even to be a boss. But God has—and Scripture clearly teaches this—given to the husband and the father in the family the responsibility of spiritual leadership. He is to be the fountainhead in that home who gives guidance and spiritual direction to the family. Some of the most aggressive feminist leaders must have married a fellow who did not take a stand. As a result, the family was a failure, and these women became bitter toward all men. There is nothing more wonderful than a godly husband who loves his wife and children and who believes that he has a lifetime commitment to them. He does not dictate to them but by example is a model for them. Macel and I have a little plaque on the dresser in our bedroom that says, "Children need models more than they need critics." That is a good saying, and that is what a husband is supposed to be. He is a model, an example, a testimony, and a spiritual leader.

In our family my wife and I are partners. I have never looked on myself as Macel's boss. I have looked on the fact that my wife and I are one. We became one flesh in marriage. How could I happily do anything that displeases her and how could she happily do anything that displeases me? I cannot think of anything of significance that either of us has ever done without agreement on both sides, and we always try to bring our children into it.

Family authority is spiritual. Some husbands and fathers do not have the respect of their families because they have not earned it. When they come home they do not have time to listen. A father should come home with love, joy, confidence, and enthusiasm. If he did that, he might be surprised how his wife and family might happily follow and emulate his example.

Family authority is important. Young people are supposed to obey their parents. Today's psychologists and sociologists are advocating rebellion on the part of children and this is tragic. Mom and Dad may not always be right, but they are always in charge. If young people honor and respect their parents, God will extend their days. To shorten their days on the earth, children need only to disrespect their parents.

Sometimes a young person will complain that his father is not a Christian. But I tell him, "He is still your dad, and the best way to win your dad to the Lord is let him see a submissive Christian child, who is obedient to authority."

Verse 15 says, "The rod and reproof give wisdom." Our friends on the left would claim that God is advocating child-beating and abuse. That is not the case at all. God says that if you want to raise up a child who will bring pleasure and blessing to you, give discipline to that child. Some have advocated that we just let children grow up and express themselves. Well, that is not the way my daddy and mom did it. When we expressed ourselves, they expressed themselves. We could feel the print for a long time, and I'm grateful for every bit of discipline I ever received from my parents. I loved them for it. The rod and reproof give wisdom.

Verse 17 says, "Correct thy son, and he shall give thee rest." That means he will give you peace in your old age. You will not be worrying about where he is. You will not be worrying about what he is doing tonight. You correct him now.

Finally, we must listen to spiritual authority. We are under family authority, but we are under spiritual authority as well. Verse 13 says, "The poor and the deceitful man meet together." That means the poor and the rich. The rich man is one who oppresses the poor. When they meet together, "the Lord lighteneth both their eyes." God gives wisdom to both the rich and the poor. Your life can be successful, no matter what your station is in life, only if you are getting wisdom from the Lord. That is because the Lord is your ultimate authority. When I got saved on January 22, 1952, Jesus became not only my Saviour, to forgive my sins and keep me out of hell, but He became the Lord of my life.

Verse 25 says, "The fear of man bringeth a snare, but whoso putteth his trust in the Lord shall be safe." Do you know what real "social security" is? A lot of older people in this country are frightened right now because we are just learning that the wild, reckless socialism of our government over the last fifty years has spent the till dry, and there is not enough money in the Social Security system to pay off. As I have said, one thing we are all learning as a nation is that there is no security on this earth as far as man is concerned.

There is only one Person who can promise you security, and that is the Lord. "Whoso putteth his trust in the Lord shall be safe" (v. 25). I can have the absolute confidence that if I live to be eighty or eighty-five, no matter what the condition of this country and our government, or the world, I have a God in heaven whose stock will still be good and whose promises are still dependable. He will take care of me and my family, my children and my grandchildren. We have a God who will make us safe if we trust Him. The only condition is that we listen to His authority.

If we desire to be successful Christians, we must see things from God's point of view. To do that, we must become good listeners. We must listen to family authority and assume the correct roles that God has given to each of us in that institution. Also, we must listen to spiritual authority. If you will practice listening in those two areas, life will be worth living. That is both the regulated and the free life in submission to the lordship of our Saviour, the Lord Jesus Christ.

12

On to
Success
Proverbs 30—31

Humility is not a virtue that is commonly applauded among men. However, Jesus commonly cited the high value that His heavenly Father places on this virtue. One of my favorite passages is 1 Peter 5:6: "Humble yourselves therefore under the mighty hand of God, that He may exalt you in due time." Here we are told to humble ourselves under the hand of God and wait for Him to exalt us. Jesus humbled Himself, and we too should be willing to put ourselves down at times in order that our Lord might lift us up.

True humility can be acquired only by the person who aspires to know God. When we realize that the Lord is in heaven and we are on earth, we ought to feel a sense of humility. Our God gathers the winds and sets the boundaries of the waters. He has established the ends of the earth.

When I think of humility, I am reminded of Isaiah's words. "In the year that King Uzziah died I saw also the Lord sitting upon a throne, high and lifted up, and His train filled the temple" (Isa. 6:1). What did this man do when he saw the

God who is high and lifted up? He did the same thing that Moses did before him and John would do after him. He fell on his face before the God of glory. He joined the heavenly throng in worship and adoration. He was totally humbled in the presence of God.

Isaiah viewed himself as unclean in the presence of God. True humility always leaves a man feeling a sense of need in the presence of the Lord. Isn't it wonderful that God has provided the blood of Jesus to cleanse us from all sin?

Humility is reinforced by learning to know the Word of God. He is a shield for those who trust in His Word. We must take care not to add to His words, or we will come under His reproof. How many times have you read your Bible through? I mean all 66 books, all 1,189 chapters. How much of the Word of God are you digesting? Knowing the Word of God by reading and digesting it will teach you true humility. When you allow the Holy Spirit to teach you, God will use the Word to point you again and again to the pathway of success.

In Proverbs 30:7-14, we are instructed that true humility is deepened when we really know ourselves. Here, the writer petitions the Lord to remove from him vanity and lies. The maintenance of humility is dependent on a biblical assessment of my need. "All have sinned, and come short of the glory of God" (Rom. 3:23). I am part of that *all.* I am likely to forget God if I have too much. If I become self-sufficient, I may find it easy to deny God a place in my life. The man of wisdom confesses his lack of character to God and waits upon the Lord to heal his waywardness.

You say, "I would never steal or lie." "The heart [of man] is ... desperately wicked: who can know it?" (Jer. 17:9) Do not say what you will or will not do. Just say, "By the grace of God I do not ever intend to do that." We need to get to that place in our individual minds where we say, "Without Him I can do nothing." There is nothing good about the flesh.

Whether it is wrapped around Jerry Falwell, or some beauty queen, or a bum on Skid Row, the flesh is not in any way serviceable for God. It is what is inside the vessel that makes the difference.

Christians have a treasure inside of them. That treasure is the indwelling Christ. His Holy Spirit causes us to triumph over the flesh, and through Him we become instruments that are useful in the work of God. Do not ever boast—pride goes before destruction.

True humility is also strengthened as we get to know God's creation. Isn't this a marvelous world that God brought into existence? Not long ago while speaking on a university campus, I had the opportunity to share ideas with some very intelligent students and faculty members. We began to talk about Creation. I suppose I was the only creationist in the group. These intellectuals began to ridicule me about why I had difficulty accepting evolution.

These evolutionists wondered why I could not see that countless years ago it all started with one little cell. They offered no explanation for the origin of this little cell. There was some difference of opinion over whether the cell was liquid, vapor, or maybe even fire. They wondered why I could not envision the process of random selection over millions of years that eventually resulted in the creation of the world as we now know it. "Why can't you accept that?" they wondered.

I replied that I just was not religious enough. It takes a terific amount of faith to believe that, and I just do not have that much faith. Frankly, it is easier for me to believe the opening verses of Genesis. I believe that our heavenly Father created it all, and I bow before Him in complete dependence and humility. A recent poll revealed that 82 percent of all Americans believe that God made this world that we are standing on.

An Insatiable Quartet

There is a circle of men who display the arrogance prayed against in Proverbs 30:7-9 and discussed in verses 11-14. The passage presents a downward spiral, as we move from the rebellious child to the brutal practices of reprobate adults. These men are consumed with pride. They are like the bloodsucking horse leech, common in Palestine. This ugly creature serves as an emblem of insatiable greed. If it could speak, it would say, "Give! Give! Give!" The leech, with its insatiable thirst for blood, serves to introduce an insatiable quartet that never have enough. "The *grave*; and the *barren womb*; the *earth* that is not filled with water; and the *fire* that saith not, It is enough" (vv. 15-16). All these are but a type of the person who restlessly mocks at his father and despises all authority. Such a person is an abomination to the Lord. In all his evil ambition he cries, "Give! Give!" The birds of heaven will feast upon his evil flesh. This too should humble man and cause him to guard his steps.

In verses 21-23, the discussion of bad things continues. Four intolerable things that cause society to tremble are now enumerated. Sudden elevation of a man of low degree to prominence can produce catastrophic results. The man who is full of himself is a cause of great mischief. The odious woman is the one who seemed destined for singleness but at last captured a man. Her conquest may go to her head. The handmaid who takes the place of her former mistress is also odious in her profuse revelry. We all remember Hagar (Gen. 16).

Proverbs 30 closes with a discussion of things that are wonderful. These things exist in stark contrast to the reprehensible things we have just considered. In verses 18-19, four marvels are enumerated. In each case it is the easy mastery of difficult things.

In verses 24-28, four things which are little upon the earth but exceedingly wise are objects of awe. The ants are little animals and are not strong. The study of the ant ought to make one believe in God. So much wisdom is programmed into their little minds. In spite of the most adverse weather conditions, they persevere. Have you ever tried to interrupt a group of ants on the march? They will go over you, around you, and through you. They will not be stopped. They know that the day of preparation comes to an end. The sun sets on opportunity. They are always prepared for winter. That is a great spiritual trait. We too should work for our God with the full knowledge that a day is coming when we will work no more.

The coneys are very weak. They are only about as big as a rabbit. This little animal is named for its habit of living in the clefts of rocks. This habit gains the coneys a high degree of security. They have no defense mechanisms—they cannot defend themselves—but they know how to hide in the rocks. We too should know how to hide in the grace of God and trust in His protective love.

The locusts model organization and discipline. They have no king, but they march in perfect order. They are committed to getting a task done and they remain in perfect fellowship for the accomplishment of their chosen goal. Christ's church should always model that same intense commitment to fellowship and the accomplishment of their appointed task.

The spider models the use of resources beyond one's own to enhance one's security and enjoyment of life. The spider shows up in the palaces of kings. He is little but he shows up in some prominent places. If we are faithful, like the little spider, we too shall be led by the Lord into some fancy places.

In verses 29-31, four creatures that are stately in their demeanor are listed. These are all meant to provide us with models that will fill us with awe and resolve. The unflinching lion is first. His boldness serves as a model for all. The greyhound models persistence and the disciplined pursuit of objectives. The hegoat is a climber, mounting ever higher. Last is the king who marches on with vigorous resolve, trampling his conquered foes.

The Godly Woman

Perhaps nothing humbles one more than a godly mother and wife. Such a woman is at the same time a source of awe. The exclamations in chapter 31 are affectionately reproachful. The mother reminds her son of truths she has taught him and the shame that will come if that instruction slips from him.

I am convinced that a Christian home is the most heavenly thing our eyes can look upon until we reach heaven itself. My mother taught me several things about being successful. For example, she taught me that to be successful in anything I must obey the moral Law of God.

● First, we must avoid premarital or extramarital sex. I am appalled to see the manner in which sexuality is exploited on television. The soap operas are often filled with illegitimate sexual activity. The amazing thing is that people get hooked on watching that type of material. Dumping that kind of garbage into the homes of America is abominable. The networks and sponsors should cut off their support for these programs. Immorality always has been and always will be wrong.

● The second moral law that must be obeyed has to do with the use of alcohol. I am a teetotaler. I am not embarrassed about that. Do you want to be a winner in life? Do not drink alcoholic beverages. Do not use drugs. Do not get involved with anything that has the ultimate power to enslave you. The drinking of wine can lead to the perversion of justice (Isa. 5:22-23). The pious women of Jerusalem used to offer wine to those condemned to crucifixion in order to deaden their misery. This was offered to the Lord Jesus (Matt.

27:34), but He refused it, for He wished to keep His mind clear to the end, as he took upon Himself the sins of all mankind. We too should face all of our realities in the power of the Holy Spirit and not look to drugs as the means by which we handle the difficult times. Certainly there will be times when the medical profession will advise medication for the proper management of a problem, but apart from that, stay away from these imprisoning narcotics.

● The third moral law is discovered in verses 8-9. The *dumb* are those timid and insecure folks who cannot get a fair hearing for themselves. Since they may be rushed by their antagonists, we have a moral obligation to speak in their behalf. As Christians we need to be possessed of a special sensitivity for pleading the cause of the poor and needy.

● The fourth moral law has to do with the requirement for honoring and elevating the virtuous woman (vv. 10-31). A society should be committed to honoring the women who model the truths expressed in Proverbs 31. The presence of women with this kind of character is an absolute necessity if a nation is to survive. Without an abundance of women with these traits, a society is doomed.

It seems that everywhere we turn today, biblical principles on the role of the mother and wife are being denigrated. Thank God there are those who still believe what Lemuel's mother taught him at her knee. George Gallup, Jr. concluded from a recent poll that 75 percent of American women still consider marriage and having children as the ideal lifestyle.

Women can have careers and still be good wives and mothers. My wife worked in a local bank until we had our first child. When our last is out and gone, she may go back to work again. I think it is great for a woman to work, but I also believe it is good for a woman to put her children ahead of her own ambitions. Women can work and have a family at the same time, but they—like their male counterparts—must be very careful to keep the priority on the home. Moms and Dads need to be more in love with each other and their children than they are with things.

Wives at home ought not to be intimidated by the feminists. Women who stay at home are not dumb or stupid and out of step—they happen to be *in* step.

The woman that builds a society is now described. I have a feeling that Lemuel is describing his own mother here. I am so glad I had the mother that I did. My wife and I both were blessed with great mothers. I have nothing but fond memories of my mother. She was first and foremost a woman of virtue.

Who can find a virtuous woman? She is of infinite value, and her husband can safely trust in her. She is a one-man woman. She cohabits with and is committed to one man for one lifetime or until death parts them. Her husband never has to wonder about whether she is unfaithful to him. He will never have to hire a detective to check up on her movements. She is trustworthy.

It is wonderful to know someone who wants to do you only good. You can really relax around a person like that. This woman desires to do her husband only good. No wonder she is trusted by her husband. Infidelity destroys the commitment to doing a partner good. Love wants to do good. Jealously and mistrust want to hurt and wound. Solomon said, "Love is strong as death; jealousy is cruel as the grave" (Song 8:6). Love, like death, is irrevocable and irreversible. You cannot buy it and you cannot kill it.

Jealousy is a tragic problem. I think we are all capable of it. When men and women go outside of marriage for affection and sex, they prove they cannot be trusted. The fruit of that deed in the life of the abandoned partner is often jealousy. Jealousy is like a cancer; it is like corruption in the body after death. It works slowly, but it eventually destroys the entire

person. Jealousy can be overcome and destroyed when husbands and wives feel the security of total commitment issuing
from their partners. The virtuous woman is committed to
commitment, and her husband can safely trust in her.

This virtuous woman is also a hard worker. She works
willingly with her hands (v. 13).

This virtuous wife is constantly increasing the substance of
her home because of the prudent care she exercises over the
available resources (vv. 14-27). She enjoys providing for her
family and therefore works uncomplainingly. Her activities
are broader than just the home. *Like the merchant ships* is
probably idiomatic for her work beyond the domestic context. She is efficient in matters of business. She is keenly alive
to the sorrows of the needy and aids them whenever it is
possible. She so enhances the performance of her husband
that he is well known in the places of leadership. Free from
domestic squabbling and uncertainty, he is able to contribute
to public life.

Such a woman is going to be an object of praise for her
husband and children (vv. 27-31). This woman is no slave to
her circumstances. She is only in bondage to her devotion to
God and her family. She has a full and beautiful life and holds
an honored place in the life of her home and community.
Charm and beauty may fade, but her resolution to fear the
Lord assures her of eternal praise. I am glad that when my
children have left our home and Mom and I are both gone,
and a reporter asks them about their mother, they can say of
her what Lemuel said of his mother. I think that is a goal
every mother should aspire to achieve.

The Book of Proverbs deals with every aspect of practical
living: raising children, husband-wife relationships,
friendships, economic and financial principles, solving personal conflicts. It is a collection of inspired sayings on how to

live successfully. Nowhere in all the world will one find better advice for life than in this book. It extols the Judeo-Christian virtues of honesty, morality, fairness, justice, work, prosperity, compassion. Proverbs is a book that has stood the test of time. For nearly 3,000 years it has remained the greatest repository of wisdom in the entire world.

Yet, there is a warning that runs throughout this book. "Why is there a price in the hand of a fool to get wisdom, seeing he hath no heart to it?" (17:16) We are living in a time of information explosion. More books are being written today than ever before in history. Computer technology has thrust us into a date-indulgent society. Yet, in spite of all this information, we are on the verge of extinction! Why? The answer of Proverbs is that while men are quick to buy information, they are slow to apply it to the development of personal character. We lack in the very area where we are strongest. Modern man without God cannot make sense of his world. He cannot figure out why he is here or what the real purpose of life is all about. It is right here, at the most crucial juncture of our lives, that God still speaks today through Proverbs. "Trust in the Lord with all thine heart; and lean not unto thine own understanding. In all thy ways acknowledge Him, and He shall direct thy paths" (3:5-6).

I would recommend that you read and reread Proverbs time and again throughout your Christian life. Here are timeless truths that can shape your life and character with godliness and practical wisdom. You will never tire of the vast treasure lying before you on these pages of Scripture. It is here in Proverbs that the wisdom of God is explained in such a way that the youngest child or eldest saint may understand. Here is truth for the newest believer or the most mature disciple. Take time to come and feast again on these wise words which shall preserve you in a wicked world.